# WHAT CHRIST THINKS OF THE CHURCH

## REVELATION 1–3 EXPOUNDED BY
# John Stott

Word (UK) Ltd
Milton Keynes, England

WORD AUSTRALIA
Kilsyth, Victoria, Australia
STRUIK CHRISTIAN BOOKS (PTY) LTD
Maitland, South Africa
ALBY COMMERCIAL ENTERPRISES PTE LTD
Balmoral Road, Singapore
CHRISTIAN MARKETING NEW ZEALAND LTD
Havelock North, New Zealand
JENSCO LTD
Hong Kong
SALVATION BOOK CENTRE
Malaysia

WORD PUBLISHING

Designed and created by
Three's Company
12 Flitcroft Street
London WC2H 8DJ

Worldwide co-edition organized
and produced by
Angus Hudson Ltd
Concorde House
Grenville Place
London NW7

Design: Peter M. Wyart
Editor: Tim Dowley

Typesetting by Watermark

Printed in Great Britain

British Commonwealth edition
published by
Word Publishing
Word (UK) Ltd
Milton Keynes
England

ISBN 0–85009–343–0

First published in the USA by
Harold Shaw Publishers
Box 567
Wheaton
Illinois 60189
USA

ISBN 0 –87788–908–2

# CONTENTS

# Preface

What Christ thinks of the church is a question of great concern to all Christians. What we ourselves think of it from the inside and what others think of it from the outside are also important. But far more significant is the view of Jesus Christ himself, since he is the church's founder, head and judge.

From every standpoint the church is an extraordinary phenomenon. From its tiny beginnings in Palestine it has developed over the centuries into a unique multi-racial, multi-national, multi-cultural community. Other religions are rightly called 'ethnic', because they are largely limited to particular peoples; only Christianity can truly be called universal, for Jesus Christ has won adherents from every race, rank and religion. Moreover, the Christian community continues to grow, in many places rapidly, even if sometimes its growth lacks depth.

So what does Christ think of his church? Fortunately we are not without the means to answer our question. For the New Testament contains much information about Christ's purposes for his people. From his own words recorded in the Gospels, from Luke's portrayal of the early church in the Acts, and from the detailed instructions of the apostles in their letters we can glean much about the nature and functions of the church.

But there is another resource at our disposal, which tends to be neglected, namely the Book of Revelation. Its second and third chapters contain seven letters, each addressed to a particular first-century Christian community in the Roman province of Asia. Although these letters were written by John, it is claimed that they were given him directly by the ascended and glorified Christ. Although their message is related to the specific situations of those churches, it expresses concerns which apply to all churches. By praise and censure, by warning and exhortation, Christ reveals what he wants his church to be like in all places and at all times.

The substance of this book was first used in embryonic form as a series of expository sermons in All Souls Church, Langham Place, London in 1957. It was then elaborated and published the following year. But now, more than 30 years later, it has been thoroughly revised, and the biblical text expounded has been changed to the New International Version.

My prayer, as this new illustrated edition appears, is that it may help church leaders to grasp where Christ's priorities lie. There is much here to call us to repentance and renewal, much to humble and shame us, much to warn us of the malice of our enemy, and much to incite us to fortitude and perseverance. May Christ speak again to our churches the truths he spoke to the churches of Asia centuries ago, and may our ears be opened to listen to 'what the Spirit is saying to the churches!'

John R.W.Stott
February 1990

*'The revelation of Jesus Christ....'*
Revelation 1:1

# INTRODUCTION

**An unfamiliar world**

Many Christians fight shy of the Book of Revelation. It seems to them wellnigh incomprehensible. They are perhaps sceptical of some fanciful interpretations they have heard, and cannot easily accustom themselves to the book's bizarre imagery. To start reading the Revelation is to step into a strange, unfamiliar world of angels and demons, of lambs, lions, horses and dragons. Seals are broken, trumpets blown, and the contents of seven bowls poured out on the earth. Two particularly malicious monsters appear, one emerging out of the sea with ten horns and seven heads, the other rising from the earth with a lamb's horns and a dragon's voice. There is thunder, lightning, hail, fire, blood and smoke. The whole book appears at first sight to contain a chaotic profusion of weird and mysterious visions.

But we cannot leave the matter there. The book claims to be a divine revelation, given by God to his servants (1:1). It promises at its beginning a special blessing to the person who reads it aloud in church and to those who listen (1:3), and it adds at the end a solemn warning to anyone who dares to tamper with its message, either by addition or by subtraction (22:18–19). Besides, this last book of the Bible has been valued by the people of God in every generation and has brought its challenge and its comfort to thousands. We would therefore be foolish to neglect it.

**Clues for interpreters**

We are concerned here with the book's first three chapters, and in particular with the second and third chapters, which contain seven letters addressed by the ascended Christ to seven churches in the Roman province of Asia. Chapter one is introductory to the whole book, and to it we now turn. Indeed, some important clues to a right interpretation of the book are given to us in its very first verse: *The revelation of Jesus Christ, which God gave him to show his servants what must soon take place. He made it known by sending his angel to his servant John.* The first word in the Greek sentence is *apocalupsis,* which (like its Latin equivalent, *revelatio*) means an 'unveiling'. The whole book is a revelation, an unveiling by God's hand of truths which would otherwise have remained hidden.

5

The revelation of Jesus Christ, which God gave him to show his servants what must soon take place. He made it known by sending his angel to his servant John, [2]who testifies to everything he saw – that is, the word of God and the testimony of Jesus Christ. [3]Blessed is the one who reads the words of this prophecy, and blessed are those who hear it and take to heart what is written in it, because the time is near.

### Greetings and Doxology

[4]John,

To the seven churches in the province of Asia:

Grace and peace to you from him who is, and who was, and who is to come, and from the seven spirits before his throne, [5]and from Jesus Christ, who is the faithful witness, the firstborn from the dead, and the ruler of the kings of the earth.

To him who loves us and has freed us from our sins by his blood, [6]and has made us to be a kingdom and priests to serve his God and Father – to him be glory and power for ever and ever! Amen.

[7]Look, he is coming with the clouds,
    and every eye will see him,
even those who pierced him;
and all the peoples of the earth will mourn
    because of him.
                    So shall it be! Amen.
[8]'I am the Alpha and the Omega,' says the Lord God, 'who is, and who was, and who is to come, the Almighty.'

### One Like a Son of Man

[9]I, John, your brother and companion in the suffering and kingdom and patient endurance that are ours in Jesus, was on the island of Patmos because of the word of God and the testimony of Jesus. [10]On the Lord's Day I was in the Spirit, and I heard behind me a loud voice like a trumpet, [11]which said: 'Write on a scroll what you see and send it to the seven churches: to Ephesus, Smyrna, Pergamum, Thyatira, Sardis, Philadelphia and Laodicea.'

[12]I turned round to see the voice that was speaking to me. And when I turned I saw seven golden lampstands, [13]and among the lampstands was someone 'like a son of man', dressed in a robe reaching down to his feet and with a golden sash round his chest. [14]His head and hair were white like wool, as white as snow, and his eyes were like blazing fire. [15]His feet were like bronze glowing in a furnace, and his voice was like the sound of rushing waters. [16]In his right hand he held seven stars, and out of his mouth came a sharp double-edged sword. His face was like the sun shining in all its brilliance.

[17]When I saw him, I fell at his feet as though dead. Then he placed his right hand on me and said: 'Do not be afraid. I am the First and the Last. [18]I am the Living One; I was dead, and behold I am alive for ever and ever! And I hold the keys of death and Hades.

[19]'Write, therefore, what you have seen, what is now and what will take place later. [20]The mystery of the seven stars that you saw in my right hand and of the seven golden lampstands is this: The seven stars are the angels of the seven churches, and the seven lampstands are the seven churches.

# A revelation to the church

It may be helpful to begin with the simple observation that the revelation was made to the church. The 'apocalypse' was given by God *to show his servants*. They were to be its recipients. It was granted for their benefit. This being so, it is absurd to give up trying to understand it. We must persevere.

In particular, the revelation which John was given and instructed to write in a book was intended for *the seven churches in the province of Asia* (verse 4). A little later he names them. He is to send the book to *Ephesus, Smyrna, Pergamum, Thyatira, Sardis, Philadelphia and Laodicea* (verse 11).

### The seven cities

The Roman province of Asia was located on the western seaboard of what we now know as Turkey. The seven cities mentioned form an irregular circle, and are listed in the order in which a messenger might visit them if commissioned to deliver the letters. Sailing from the island of Patmos, to which John had been banished, he would arrive at Ephesus. He would then travel north to Smyrna and Pergamum, south-east to Thyatira, Sardis and Philadelphia, and finish his journey at Laodicea. He would need only to keep to what the British archaeologist Sir William Ramsay called 'the great circular road that bound together the most populous, wealthy and influential part of the Province, the west-central region'.

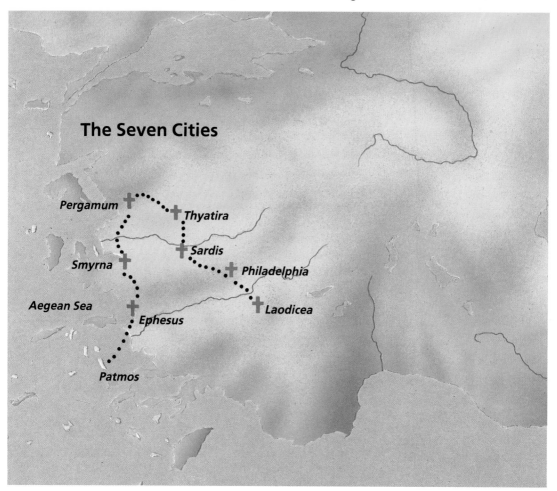

**The Seven Cities**

Pergamum

Thyatira

Sardis

Smyrna

Philadelphia

Aegean Sea

Laodicea

Ephesus

Patmos

This historical context for the Book of Revelation, however, cannot possibly be thought to exhaust its significance. Just as the letters of Paul to (for example) the Corinthians and the Thessalonians convey the word of God to us as well as to them, to London, New York and Cairo as well as to Corinth and Thessalonica, so Christ's letters through John to the first-century Christian communities of Asia have a permanent value and a universal message. Commentators have not failed to notice that the Asian churches numbered seven, a number indicating perfection and completeness in a book whose numerals are nearly always symbolical. The seven churches of Asia, though historical, represent the local churches of all ages and of all lands.

### Systematic persecution

The Christian society in the Roman province of Asia at that time was hard pressed. It is probable that the Revelation reflects the situation during the reign of the Emperor Domitian (AD 81–96), who carried to its second stage the persecution of Christians begun twenty-five years previously by Nero. Nero's persecutions had been sporadic; Domitian's seem to have been more systematic. The effects of Nero's antagonism were felt in Rome only, while under Domitian, who was hungry for divine honours, the persecution spread to Asia. Christians who worshipped the Lord Christ were being invited to worship the Lord Caesar. The battle was joined. The hearts of Christian people were filled with alarm. Already some of their number were receiving personal insults. Others were being boycotted in business. One or two had even lost their lives. Could the church survive the storm which seemed to be on the point of breaking?

Persecution was not the only peril to which the churches of Asia were exposed. There was also error to be refuted and evil to be overcome. False prophets were abroad, who were contriving to deceive even established Christians by their heretical philosophies. Immoral men and women too were contaminating the church by their influence, and standards of behaviour were being lowered.

### The devil's tactics

Persecution, error and sin. These were not inexplicable phenomena. John recognized their source with a clarity of insight which we badly need to recapture today. The devil was at work. Behind the outward situation in the Asian churches an invisible conflict raged between Christ and Antichrist, between the Lamb and the Dragon, between 'the holy city' Jerusalem (the church) and 'the great city' Babylon (the

world). The devil's assault upon Christ's church was a multiple movement. He attacked from several directions. Now the onslaught was physical, through a persecuting emperor and his deputies. Now it was intellectual, through false cults, and now moral, through sub-Christian ethical standards. These were the devil's three strategies, symbolically represented in the Revelation as the dragon's three allies: the beast from the sea, the beast from the earth (or the false prophet) and the harlot.

In every age it has been the same. The devil's tactics do not change. As we look round the world today, the same pressures are harassing different churches. In some areas of the world open hostility to the gospel is accompanied by physical violence. In others, the church is wrestling in intellectual combat with an insidious ideology or a materialistic philosophy with which it cannot come to terms. Elsewhere the struggle is in the moral field, as the world seeks to cajole the church into conformity to its own ways.

The Book of Revelation begins to be intelligible only when it is seen as God's word to his servants in this situation. It is a message to the church in the world. It is a call to us to endure tribulation, to hold fast to the truth, to resist the blandishments of the devil and to obey the commandments of God.

# A revelation of Jesus Christ

If the recipients of the revelation are the churches of Christ, the substance of the revelation is Christ himself. The book begins by describing itself as *the revelation of Jesus Christ*, and ends in its last two verses with echoes of his name (Revelation 22:20,21). To call it 'the Revelation of St John the Divine', as is often done, is thoroughly misleading. The revelation is indeed given *to* John; but it is *of* Christ. He is himself its grand theme.

### A vision of Christ
A church with its back to the wall, fighting for survival, needs more than moral exhortation and pious entreaty; it must see Christ. A history of the world in cipher (which some believe the Revelation to be) is cold comfort in comparison with a vision of the exalted Christ. The whole book concerns him. Nobody can read it without gaining a clearer view of him.

The first chapter makes this fact particularly plain. When Jesus Christ is introduced, he is given an impressive list of three titles, to which is added a statement both of his past achievement and of his future triumph (verses 5–7). First, he is *the faithful witness*. Is the church called to bear witness in the world? Let it follow the example of its Lord. He said he had come into the world to bear witness to the truth (John 18:37), and throughout his ministry he was faithful. He spoke of what he knew and bore witness to what he had seen, and 'while testifying before Pontius Pilate made the good confession' (John 3:11; 1 Timothy 6:13). He never faltered, even when he suffered. We must be faithful in our witness too.

Next, he is called *the firstborn from the dead.* Others had been brought back to this life, but he was the first to be raised to a new and indestructible life. Others had returned to life, only to die again. He rose and is *alive for ever and ever.* He is now *the Living One* (verse 18); death has no further dominion over him. A persecuted church facing the possibility of martyrdom urgently needs this assurance.

Thirdly, he is named *ruler of the kings of the earth* (verse 5). Earthly kings might seek to crush the church, but Jesus Christ is the King of kings. Human lords might try to domineer the lives of Christians, but Christ is the Lord of lords. He directs the affairs and destinies of nations. He rules the kings on earth. His empire is wider than the sway of Rome. His dominion is universal.

**Ruins of the Double Church, or Church of the Virgin Mary, Ephesus.**

## A doxology

To these three titles John adds in an eloquent doxology a description of our Lord's achievements, past and future. Not only does he love us; not only has he *freed us from our sins by his blood* (verse 5); but he has *made us to be a kingdom* (verse 6). Just as God entered into a covenant with the Israelites at Mount Sinai and made them his people, his kingdom over whom he ruled, so Christ by his death has ratified a new covenant and inaugurated a new kingdom. The Christian church is the new theocracy. Christ reigns over us. We are his kingdom. Moreover, as in the old Israel so in the new, the members of God's kingdom are *priests,* enjoying intimate access to him and offering him the spiritual sacrifice of our worship.

He who has redeemed us and made us a kingdom and priests is one day *coming with the clouds, and every eye will see him, even those who pierced him; and all the peoples of the earth will mourn because of him* (verse 7). The eyes that now view him with contempt will see him then with terror. He is coming in judgment. He will put wrongs to right and redress the uneven balance of this present world. Let Christians lift up their heads! The day of their redemption is near.

Such is the opening revelation of Jesus Christ in his titles and his deeds. It is a foretaste of the richer disclosures which follow.

John goes on to write how on a certain Sunday during his exile he was granted a vision of Jesus. He describes the details of what he saw, each part of which is meaningful. At the same time, it is important to remember that the imagery he uses is intended to be symbolical rather than pictorial. The various elements of the vision are significant symbols to be interpreted, rather than actual features to be imagined. For example, if John saw Jesus with a sharp two-edged sword issuing from his mouth, we are not so much to visualize this literally as to remember that the words which Christ speaks are as sharp and piercing as a sword.

## 'Like a son of man'

John's attention was drawn to the presence of Jesus by a loud voice behind him. Turning round, he *saw seven golden lampstands* and in the middle of them *someone 'like a son of man'* (verses 12, 13). That is to say, he saw a human figure, although the person he saw was more than a mere man. He was glorious and sublime. He was like the son of man in Daniel's vision (see Daniel 7:13,14). He was in fact the glorified 'man Christ Jesus'. John at once noticed his clothes, for he was invested with the long robe and golden girdle of a priest, king or judge. His appearance was not only distin-

The Byzantine basilica of St John at Selçuk, near ancient Ephesus.

guished but venerable and holy, for his hair was as white as wool or snow. His scrutiny was intense, as his eyes flashed with the fire of judgment, and his feet were as strong as burnished brass. His voice thundered like the breakers which dashed themselves against the rocky coast of Patmos, and his face was as radiant as the sun (verses 13–15).

The purpose of this vision was not the private enlightenment of John, however. The seer was to be allowed no personal monopoly of its riches. The vision was for the whole church. John was given it in order to transmit it to others. *'Write on a scroll what you see,'* he was told, *'and send it to the seven churches ...'* (verse 11).

This visionary manifestation of Christ was too much for John to endure. It had been deafening to his ears and dazzling to his eyes. He *fell at his feet as though dead* (verse 7). But Jesus laid his hand on John's shoulder and said to him reassuringly, *'Do not be afraid'.*

13

### Seven lampstands

Rising to his feet, John could now absorb the immediate message which Christ had to convey. The Lord affirmed his victory over death, commanded John to write in a book what he had seen and would yet see (verses 18,19), and then interpreted the two most prominent features of the vision, which I have not yet mentioned. These concern the seven lampstands among which Jesus stood, and the seven stars which he held in his right hand. Indeed, when John first turned round and saw the vision, it was on the lampstands rather than on Christ that his eyes fell (verse 12). He did not see a candelabrum consisting of one lampstand with seven branches (such as stood in the tabernacle outside the veil). He saw seven separate lampstands, each no doubt with a lighted lamp, and Jesus Christ among them. *The seven lampstands,* Jesus explained, stood for *the seven churches,* and *the seven stars* for *the angels of the seven churches* (verse 20).

What these 'angels' were, we cannot say for certain. They may have been the heavenly representatives and guardians of the churches, or perhaps the presiding ministers or 'bishops' of the churches. What is clear is that both stars and lamps diffuse light, even if in differing degrees. So Christ's churches are meant to be light-bearers in the darkness of the world. No one can disperse the shadows of sin and sorrow but he who is the Light of the World and those to whom he gave his own title. 'You are the light of the world', he said in the Sermon on the Mount, '...let your light shine ...' (John 8:12; Matthew 5:14,16). But the church's light is as borrowed as the moon's. If the stars are to shine and the lamps are to burn, they must remain in Christ's hand and in Christ's presence.

# A revelation through John

Our account of the first chapter of the Revelation would not be complete if we gave the impression that Christ's message to the church was immediate and direct. It was not. It was given through John. It was indeed a revelation of Christ to his church, but John was the means of its transmission. *He made it known ... to his servant John* (verse 1). Christ's command to him to write the visions in a book and send it to the seven churches is repeated twice (verses 11 and 19) and occurs again at the threshold of each separate letter.

### Who is John?

Scholars continue to debate the identity of the human author of the Revelation. In this book I am assuming the traditional view that the writer who describes himself as plain 'John', without any further clarification, is the apostle, the beloved disciple, the son of Zebedee and brother of James, who survived the other apostles and lived to a ripe old age as leader of the church at Ephesus. Certainly the author of Revelation possesses an authority which the churches of Asia recognized and is familiar with their geographical, social and spiritual condition.

His relationship with them is made closer by his sufferings. *I, John,* he writes, am *your brother and companion in the suffering and kingdom and patient endurance that are ours in Jesus* (verse 9). He is on the island of Patmos, neither as a visitor nor as a missionary, but as an exile. To this 'barren, rocky island about ten miles long and five wide' (R.H.Charles) he has been banished *because of the word of God and the testimony of Jesus.* He has been bold in his preaching and faithful in his witness, and he has had to suffer for it. He has not escaped the tribulation which is engulfing the churches of Asia. But if he shares the suffering, he shares the glory too. He knows himself to be already a member of Christ's kingdom, just as they are, and he is learning the same constancy and fortitude in his trial which he earnestly desires for them.

It is to such a man, called, chosen and faithful, a partaker of Christ's sufferings, kingdom and patience, that this wonderful revelation is given. It is a disclosure of Christ through his servant John to the churches.

### Christ's view of his church
What Christ thinks of his church and what he says to it we shall discover in detail in the next chapters. He has a right to think and say what he does. In the first place, it is his church. He founded it on the rock and promised that the gates of hell would not prevail against it (Matthew 16:18). He is its head and the source of its life. In the second place, he knows it intimately. In each of the seven letters he begins 'I know'. 'I know your deeds, your hard work and your perseverance', he says. 'I know your affliction and your poverty'. 'I know where you live.' 'I know ... your love and faith, your service and perseverance' (2:2,9,13,19). He walks among the lampstands, patrolling and supervising his churches. He is the chief pastor of his people.

What then is his view of his church? In each of the letters which follow, the risen Lord lays emphasis, either in rebuke or in commendation, on one particular aspect of an ideal church. Put together, these characteristics constitute the seven marks of a true and living church. They tell us what Christ thinks of his church, both as it is and as it should be.

*'You have forsaken your first love.'*
Revelation 2:4

## The Letter to Ephesus:

# Love
Revelation 2:1–7

### Ephesus

The first of the seven letters is addressed to the church in Ephesus, if for no better reason than because it was nearer to the island of Patmos than the other six cities. A straight sail of sixty miles would bring the bearer of the letter to the port of Ephesus at the mouth of the River Cayster.

But Ephesus was more than the nearest city to Patmos. It had a distinction of its own. Its citizens liked to call it 'the metropolis of Asia', and indeed it was the capital of the Roman Province. It was also a prosperous business centre, particularly because it was situated on the trade route from Rome to the

**Inset: The Street of the Curetes, Ephesus; the Library of Celsus may be seen in the distance.**

## Revelation 2:1–7

'To the angel of the church in Ephesus write:

These are the words of him who holds the seven stars in his right hand and walks among the seven golden lampstands: ²I know your deeds, your hard work and your perseverance. I know that you cannot tolerate wicked men, that you have tested those who claim to be apostles but are not, and have found them to be false. ³You have persevered and have endured hardships for my name, and have not grown weary.

⁴Yet I hold this against you: You have forsaken your first love. ⁵Remember the height from which you have fallen! Repent and do the things you did at first. If you do not repent, I will come to you and remove your lampstand from its place. ⁶But you have this in your favour: You hate the practices of Nicolaitans, which I also hate.

⁷He who has an ear, let him hear what the Spirit says to the churches. To him who overcomes, I will give the right to eat from the tree of life, which is in the paradise of God.

east. Its magnificent Ionic temple in honour of Diana, or Artemis, was acknowledged as one of the seven wonders of the world.

### Paul and Ephesus
The apostle Paul had been frustrated in his attempt to visit Ephesus when outward bound on his second missionary journey. We do not know the circumstances, but according to Luke's narrative he was 'kept by the Holy Spirit from preaching the word in the province of Asia' (Acts 16:6).

On his return journey however Paul paid Ephesus a brief visit and evidently recognized its strategic importance so clearly that he went straight back to it on his third journey and spent at least two and a half years in the city. He gave public lectures and visited people privately in their homes, and the gospel spread throughout the whole neighbourhood. In the end a riot broke out over the drop in sales of silver models of Diana's temple. The uproar is vividly described by Luke in Acts 19.

### Timothy and John
Later, after Paul had left Ephesus, he put Timothy in charge of the church, to supervise the growing work and to guard the truth of the gospel. From his first imprisonment in Rome he wrote his letter to the Ephesian church, and later still his two letters to Timothy.

According to an early tradition, the apostle John replaced Timothy towards the end of the first century as leader of the Ephesian church, and probably addressed his first letter to them. Now John is in exile for the truth, but is given the opportunity to write to his beloved church a letter which is dictated to him by Jesus Christ.

# A commendation

In each of the seven letters Jesus Christ passes a moral judgment upon the church concerned. To the church in Smyrna he gives unmixed praise, while to the church in Laodicea he expresses unrelieved condemnation. The Philadelphian church is more praised than blamed, the church in Sardis more blamed than praised, while in the letters to Ephesus, Pergamum and Thyatira, approval and disapproval are fairly evenly balanced.

It is clear that the risen Lord is in a position to evaluate the condition of each church and to commend or condemn it, for he knows its state with perfect accuracy. We have already seen that every letter is introduced by the statement 'I know'. Of course he knows. As he says here, it is he *who holds the seven stars in his right hand and walks among the seven golden lampstands* (verse 1).

The claim is even stronger now than the earlier one in the first chapter. He not only 'has' the stars; he holds them. He not only stands in the midst of the lampstands; he walks among them. He is the divine overseer of the churches. Did he not say 'where two or three come together in my name, there am I with them' (Matthew 18:20)? Christ visits his people. He dwells with them. He walks among them. He inspects them. He knows them.

**The church at Ephesus exhibited three virtues which Jesus Christ could commend without qualification.**

### The church's deeds
*I know your deeds,* he says, and immediately adds by way of explanation, *your hard work.* The Ephesian church was an active church, busy in the service of God and human beings. One may imagine that its members were fully occupied in entertaining the lonely, nursing the sick, teaching the young and visiting the aged. No doubt some gave hours of their time to making and mending for the church. Perhaps others spent their leisure hours writing or cooking, cleaning or organizing. The church of Ephesus was a veritable beehive of industry. Their toil was famous. Every member was doing something for Christ. They were diligent and conscientious.

### The church's endurance
The Christians in Ephesus had evidently been exposed to some fierce local opposition. The city was a meeting place of many religions. It was one of the great centres of emperor worship in the province. Some of its inhabitants practised magical arts from the East, while everybody had a profound reverence for the great Diana of the Ephesians, the mother goddess of Asia, on account of whom the city had been put in a ferment through the apostle Paul's preaching. Craftsmen feared for their sales of silver shrines, and their vested interests led them to oppose Paul violently (see Acts 19).

Paul had left Ephesus and died long ago, but the unpopularity of the Christians still lingered. They knew what it was to be hated, to be snubbed in public and maligned in private. Some found business hard, since they were losing customers. Others found shopping a problem, as a number of tradesmen would not sell to them.

John was to describe later in his book how through the influence of the 'false prophet' (or 'beast from the earth') no one could buy or sell unless they bore on them the mark of the beast

(Revelation 13:17). This probably means that those who would not indulge in the popular worship of the emperor (or perhaps of Diana) were boycotted. There had even perhaps been physical violence to endure, as well as social ostracism.

Nevertheless, despite all this tribulation, the Ephesians had not denied Christ. They were firm and unswerving in their allegiance to him. *I know ... your perseverance* (verse 2), he says to them. This was their second characteristic.

### The church's orthodoxy

The third virtue which Christ could unreservedly praise in Ephesus was their orthodox faith. They had been visited by some self-styled apostles who were called (either by themselves, by others or by John) *Nicolaitans* (verse 6). Exactly who they were and what they taught it is not possible to say with any dogmatism. Some of the early Church Fathers believed that they were disciples of Nicolas of Antioch, 'a convert to Judaism', who is mentioned in Acts 6:5 as one of the seven chosen to help the apostles in practical ministry.

This may or may not be so. It is enough here to know that their teaching was seriously mistaken, especially in condoning immorality. Archbishop R.C.Trench thought that their name is symbolical, like the rest of the names in the book of Revelation, and pointed out that the Greek word *Nikolaos* means 'Destroyer of the People', an apt epithet for this harmful sect. They were spreading their evil doctrines throughout the churches of Asia. They are mentioned again by name in the letter to Pergamum, where we shall consider their teaching in greater detail, and probably by implication in the letters to Thyatira and Sardis as well.

Paul had warned the elders of the Ephesian church that such an invasion by heretical teachers would take place. During his voyage to Palestine at the end of his third missionary journey, his ship had put in at Miletus, thirty-five miles away, and he had sent for them to come to him. In his charge to them, he said: 'I know that after I leave, savage wolves will come in among you and will not spare the flock. Even from your own number men will arise and distort the truth in order to draw away disciples after them' (Acts 20:29–30). Now the wolves had come. Ravenous beasts had got into the sheepfold. False prophets were insinuating their dark and dangerous doctrines among the people of God.

What did the Ephesian Christians do in this situation? At first they listened. They could not tell whether the teaching of the Nicolaitans came from a human source, or from Satan, or from God, until they had given it a fair hearing. But as they heard it, they sifted it. They 'tested the spirits', to see whether they were from God (1 John 4:1). They were determined to 'test everything', so that they might hold on to what was good, and avoid every kind of evil (1 Thessalonians 5:21–2). No doubt they thought, prayed and discussed. They will also have searched the scriptures and compared the teaching of these vaunted apostles with the original apostolic message which they had received. Then, after an honest hearing and a careful testing, they absolutely rejected what the Nicolaitans taught.

They *tested those who claim to be apostles but are not, and found them to be false* (verse 2). It was not just the belief of the Nicolaitans which was faulty, but also their behaviour. Jesus himself had said that a prophet could be recognized by his works, as a tree is told by its fruit. So the Ephesians examined the works of the Nicolaitans and came to detest them. *But you have this in your favour,* said the risen Jesus in his commendation, *you hate the practices of the Nicolaitans, which I also hate* (verse 6).

The Ephesians had not been deceived. They possessed the rare gift of discernment. They were discriminating. Their orthodoxy was unimpaired. They were not so stupid as to suppose that Christian charity can tolerate false apostles. True love embraces neither error nor evil. I trust they did not hate the Nicolaitans; but they hated their works, and utterly repudiated them.

### A pure church
A few years later this church was still renowned for its doctrinal purity. Bishop Ignatius of Antioch wrote to them at the beginning of the second century: 'You all live according to truth, and no heresy has a home among you; indeed, you do not so much as listen to anyone if they speak of anything except concerning Jesus Christ in truth.'

What a splendid church the Christian community in Ephesus seemed to be! It appeared to be a model church in every way. Its members were busy in their service, patient in their sufferings, and orthodox in their belief. What more could be asked of them? Only one thing was lacking, and Jesus Christ lays his finger gently on it. In doing so, he is obliged to turn from commendation to complaint.

# A complaint

*Yet this I hold against you: You have forsaken your first love* (verse 4). They had fallen from the early heights of their devotion and had descended to the plains of mediocrity. In a word, they were backsliders. Did not Jesus himself prophesy that when wickedness multiplies, 'the love of most will grow cold'

(Matthew 24:12)? Certainly the hearts of the Ephesian Christians had chilled.

The words of Christ's complaint do not themselves make clear whether the first love which they had abandoned was love for him or love for their fellow human beings, but the analogy with the Old Testament makes the former almost certain.

### God's bride

God often likened Israel to his bride and himself to her husband. He had set his love upon her. When she was 'at the age for love' (Ezekiel 16:8), he had taken her to himself. He had pledged his loyalty to her and entered into a covenant with her. But alas! She began to flirt with other lovers, the Canaanite gods. She played the harlot with them. She became unfaithful and forsook her true husband. So Jeremiah proclaimed the word of the Lord in the hearing of the inhabitants of Jerusalem: 'I remember the devotion of your youth, how as a bride you loved me and followed me through the desert, through a land not sown' (Jeremiah 2:2).

In the New Testament God's new Israel (the church) is similarly represented as married to Christ, just as the old Israel was married to Jehovah. 'I promised you to one husband, to Christ,' Paul wrote to the Corinthians, 'so that I might present you as a pure virgin to him. But I am afraid that as Eve was deceived by the serpent's cunning, your minds will be led astray from your sincere and pure devotion to Christ' (2 Corinthians 11:2,3). It was this very tendency which was apparent at Ephesus, and the Heavenly Bridegroom had to complain of it. Their first flush of ecstasy had passed. Their early devotion to Christ had cooled. They had been in love with him, but now they had fallen out of love.

### First love

So the Bridegroom seeks to woo his bride back to her first love. With the same tenderness that Jehovah showed to fickle, adulterous Israel, the Lord Jesus appeals to his church to return to him. The prophet Hosea, who had learned through the agony of his own wife's unfaithfulness how unquenchable is the love of God, conveyed God's word to the old Israel: 'Behold I will allure her, and bring her into the wilderness, and speak tenderly to her ... and there she shall answer as in the days of her youth, as at the time when she came out of the land of Egypt. And in that day ... you will call me "My husband" ...' Again 'I will betroth you to me for ever; I will betroth you to me in righteousness and in justice, in steadfast love, and in mercy. I will betroth you to me in faithfulness; and you shall know the Lord' (Hosea 2:14–16; 19–20).

**The site of the great Artemision, or Temple of Diana, Ephesus, now a muddy swamp. The single column has been rebuilt in recent times.**

The Divine Lover still sorrows when his love is unrequited, and pines for our continuing, deepening, maturing adoration. Love, then, is the first mark of a true and living church. Indeed, it is not a living church at all unless it is a loving church. The Christian life is essentially a love-relationship to Jesus Christ. 'Jesus captured me,' wrote Wilson Carlile, founder and 'chief' of the Church Army. 'For me to know Jesus is a love affair.'

### Undying love

Without this love, the church's work is lifeless. It is significant that the apostle Paul had ended his letter to the Ephesians with a special prayer for all those 'who love our Lord Jesus Christ with love undying' (Ephesians 6:24). Some thirty years had passed since then. A new generation had arisen in the Ephesian church, which did not heed this warning. Their love was faltering, weakening, dying. The tide of devotion had turned and was ebbing fast. They toiled with vigour, but not with love. They endured with fortitude but without love. They tested the message of their teachers, but had no love in their hearts.

However, toil becomes drudgery if it is not a labour of love. Jacob could work seven years for the hand of Rachel only because he loved her, and the seven years 'seemed to him but a few days because of the love he had for her' (Genesis 29:20). The endurance of suffering can be hard and bitter if it is not softened and sweetened by love. It is one thing to grit our teeth and clench our fists with Stoical indifference, but quite another to smile in the face of adversity with Christian love. As for orthodoxy, it is cold and dead without the warmth and beauty with which love invests it. The Ephesians even hated the evil deeds and words of the Nicolaitans, so unimpeachable was their theological correctness, but to hate error and evil is not the same as to love Christ.

### The greatest thing in the world

Again and again the New Testament reiterates its emphasis on the pre-eminence of love. In Professor Henry Drummond's famous phrase, it is 'the greatest thing in the world'. Indeed, it is the greatest thing in the universe. The first two commandments are to love God and our neighbour. So, to love is to fulfil the law.

Love is greater than knowledge, asserts Paul in his first letter to the Corinthians, because whereas knowledge puffs up, love builds up. Knowledge can merely inflate the clever person with wind, while love develops solid character. Besides, knowledge concerns things, whereas love concerns persons, including the person of God; and the knowledge of a doctrine is a one-sided, static affair, while love is reciprocal and growing (1 Corinthians 8:1–3).

Love is greater even than faith and hope (1 Corinthians 13:13), for love is everlasting and indestructible. 'Love never ends'.

## A concluding command

Jesus Christ is not content to leave the church of Ephesus, nor any church, wandering in the deserts of lovelessness. He will recall her to her senses. He will bring her back to the oases of love. So he issues to the Ephesian church three terse words of command (verse 5).

### Remember

First, the church is commanded to remember its former condition. *Remember the height from which you have fallen!* Memory is a precious gift. To look back can be sinful; but it can also be sensible. To look back with lustful eyes, as Lot's wife did, to the sins of Sodom from which we have been delivered, is to court disaster. To look back wistfully to the easy-going comforts of the world once we have put our hand to the plough is to be unfit for the Kingdom of God. But to look back along the way that God has led us is the least that gratitude can do, and to look back to the spiritual heights which once by the grace of God we occupied is to take the first step along the road of repentance. We must not live in the past. But to recall it, and to compare what we are with what we were, is a salutary, and often disturbing, experience.

## Repent

Secondly, the church is commanded to *repent,* which means to change direction. It is resolutely and completely to turn one's back on all known sin. Jesus Christ does not ask us to conjure up an emotional experience. He does not urge the Ephesian Christians to feel bad about their sins. It is not what they feel about them which matters, so much as what they do about them. They must not wait till they feel sorry. The fact is they have sinned, and they must turn from their sin in repentance. There is no need to wait. They must first recall what has been good in their past and then reject what has been wrong. Let them confess their loss of love and give it up.

How sane and matter-of-fact is this word of Christ! So many of us admit our present state, but wait for some emotional upheaval to set us right. We are like children who fall in a puddle and sit in the mud waiting for someone to pick them up. But they should get up at once. So should we, just as soon as we are conscious of having fallen.

## Resume

Thirdly, the church is commanded to resume its former state. *Do the things you did at first.* Again, there is no waiting. There is no suggestion that, having fallen out of love with Christ, they must delay until they have fallen in love with him again. Having abandoned their first love, they must go back to it. By God's grace it is in their power to do so. They have fallen from the heights of love; let them take them by storm again. They have lost what once they had; they must recapture it. 'Renew your early devotion to me,' says Christ; 'resume the work you used to do.' The work will be the same as it was during the intervening period of lovelessness, or similar. But there will be a new vigour in the doing of it, a new singleness of mind and purity of motive, a new secret of joyful perseverance in the face of many trials, and a new care even for those whose false words and evil deeds the Ephesians would continue rightly to hate. Love will cause a transformation scene on the stage of Ephesus.

Jesus Christ does not simply issue commands; he enforces them with strong arguments, and with these this brief letter closes. He adds to his instruction a solemn warning and a gracious promise.

## A solemn warning

He warns them that if they disobey his commands and do not repent, their church's existence will be ignominiously terminated. *If you do not repent, I will come to you and remove your lampstand from its place* (verse 5). No church has a secure and permanent place in the world. It is continuously on trial. If we can judge from the letter which Bishop Ignatius of Antioch wrote to the Ephesian church at the beginning of the second century, it rallied after Christ's appeal. For Ignatius described it in glowing terms. But later it lapsed again, and by the Middle Ages its Christian testimony had been obliterated. A traveller visiting the village 'found only three Christians there', wrote Archbishop Trench, 'and these sunken in such ignorance and apathy as scarcely to have heard the names of St Paul or St John.'

Christ's warning to Ephesus is just as appropriate to us today. Our own church's light will be extinguished if we stubbornly persevere in our refusal to love Christ. The church has no light without love. Only when its love burns can its light shine. Many churches today have ceased truly to exist. Their buildings may remain intact, their ministers minister and their congregations congregate, but their lampstand has been removed. The church is plunged in darkness. No glimmer of light radiates from it. It has no light, because it has no love. Let us heed this warning before it is too late.

**A promise to the penitent**
To this warning for the impenitent, Christ adds a promise to the penitent. *To him who overcomes, I will give the right to eat from the tree of life, which is in the paradise of God* (verse 7). Each of the seven letters ends with a promise to the conqueror, to the person, that is, who obeys the message of the letter and overcomes in the conflict with evil. The promise in this case is particularly apt. It offers free access to the tree of life in God's paradise, whose fruit was previously forbidden to fallen human beings. This means the enjoyment of eternal life in heaven. But what is eternal life if it is not to know and love God and his Son Jesus Christ (John 17:3)? And what is heaven but the abode of love? For heaven is where God is, and God is love. So the reward of love is more love in the perfect communion of heaven.

No hint is given in this letter as to how love may be quickened, but John tells us the way in his first letter. 'We love,' he writes, 'because he first loved us' (1 John 4:19). This prior love of God took Christ to the cross to die for our sins. There he gave himself for us with the absolute self-giving of love, as he bore our sins in his own body. 'This is how we know what love is: Jesus Christ laid down his life for us' (1 John 3:16). The cross is the blazing fire at which the flame of our love is kindled, but we have to get near enough to it for its sparks to fall on us.

So the church today, like the church of Ephesus, has a work to be done, a fight to be fought and a creed to be championed. But above all it has a person to be loved, with the love we had for him at first, a 'love undying'.

*'I know your afflictions.... Do not be
afraid of what you are about to suffer.'*
Revelation 2:9,10

The Letter to Smyrna:

# Suffering

Revelation 2:8–11

If the first mark of a true and living church is love, the second
is suffering. The one is naturally consequent on the other. A
willingness to suffer proves the genuineness of love. We are
willing to suffer for those we love. Evidently Christians in
Smyrna had not lost their pristine love for Christ, as had the
Christians in Ephesus, for they were prepared to suffer for him.
Like Peter and John, they were 'rejoicing because they had
been counted worthy of suffering disgrace for the Name [that
is, Christ's name]' (Acts 5:41).

   The town of Smyrna (modern Izmir) is situated about thirty-
five miles up the coast from, and almost due north of, Ephesus.
It was the next city the postman would reach on his circular
tour of the seven churches. Commentators describe it as the
most splendid of the seven cities. It boasted of being 'the pride
of Asia' and was sensitive to the rivalry of Ephesus. A fine road
gave it access to the interior, and its excellent natural harbour
commanded a flourishing export trade. It was 'one of the most
prosperous cities in Asia Minor' (R.H.Charles).

   We do not know when the church of Smyrna was founded.
It is mentioned neither in the Acts nor in the New Testament
letters, although an early tradition states that the apostle Paul
visited the town on his way to Ephesus at the beginning of his
third missionary tour.

   What was the ascended Lord's message to his servants in
Smyrna?

## The sufferings they endured for Christ

The church of Smyrna was a suffering church, and this letter is
devoted exclusively to an account of their past and present
afflictions, a warning of severer trials to come, and encourage-
ments to endure.

## Revelation 2:8–11

'To the angel of the church in Smyrna write:

These are the words of him who is the First and the Last, who died and came to life again. ⁹I know your afflictions and your poverty – yet you are rich! I know the slander of those who say they are Jews and are not, but are a synagogue of Satan. ¹⁰Do not be afraid of what you are about to suffer. I tell you, the devil will put some of you in prison to test you, and you will suffer persecution for ten days. Be faithful, even to the point of death, and I will give you the crown of life.

¹¹He who has an ear, let him hear what the Spirit says to the churches. He who overcomes will not be hurt at all by the second death.

Inset: The Agora, or marketplace, Izmir (ancient Smyrna), built on the orders of Alexander the Great.

*I know your affliction* (verse 9). Clearly this was persecution. The church was up against it. The enemies of the faith were aggressive and cruel. It was a dangerous thing to be a Christian in Smyrna. There was no knowing what might happen to the followers of Jesus Christ.

### Christ and Caesar

The causes of the persecution are not given, but we can tentatively reconstruct the situation. Already in 195 BC a temple to *Dea Roma*, Rome personified as a goddess, had been built and dedicated in Smyrna, and the city had acquired a reputation for its patriotic loyalty to the Empire. Round about the year AD 25 many Asian cities were competing with one another for the coveted favour of erecting a temple to the Emperor Tiberius, and the privilege was granted to Smyrna alone. Evidently then the cult of Empire and Emperor, of Rome and Rome's Caesar, was a matter of great pride in Smyrna. Did the Christians refuse to sprinkle incense on the fire which burned before the emperor's bust? Of course they did. To do so would be idolatry. They could not call Caesar Lord when Jesus was their Lord. But their unwillingness to conform was interpreted by others as a disgraceful lack of patriotism, and even as treachery.

Popular antagonism to the Christians for their refusal to take part in emperor worship was also fanned into flame by the Jewish population. They were themselves exempt from all sacrificial obligations, and they seem to have exploited their privilege by harrying the hated Nazarenes (Christians). Suspect on account of their own refusal to sacrifice, they perhaps curried favour with the authorities and the people by urging the Christians to sacrifice and vilifying them if they would not.

**Jewish opposition**
This Jewish opposition, so bitter and vociferous in demanding from Pilate the crucifixion of Jesus, had dogged the footsteps of Paul throughout his missionary expeditions. It was the Jews who were jealous of the crowds when they thronged to hear him in Pisidian Antioch and who incited some of the leading men and women to drive him and Barnabas out of the city. They then pursued him to Iconium, and on to Lystra, where they persuaded the people to stone him. In Thessalonica they caused a riot, and in Corinth they so vigorously opposed the gospel that Paul 'shook out his clothes in protest and said to them, "Your blood be on your own heads! I am clear of my responsibility. From now on I will go to the Gentiles"' (Acts 18:6). When he was back in Jerusalem, they arrested him in the temple and nearly killed him. When this attempt failed, they did their best by secret plots and public accusations to have him put to death. The Book of Acts ends with him in Rome still disputing with Jewish leaders, and accusing them of being culpably blind and deaf (see Acts 13:45,50; 14:2,5,19; 17:5–7; 18:5,6; 21:27; 25:12; 28:17–28).

This Jewish hostility to the gospel was also seen in the middle of the second century AD when in this same town of Smyrna its saintly Bishop Polycarp was martyred. A description of this will be given later, but it may be mentioned now that it was the Jews who cried loudest that he should be thrown to the lions; and when the order was finally given for him to be burned alive, it was again the Jews who were the most diligent of the crowd to fetch faggots for the fatal wood-pile.

**What form did the persecution take in Smyrna? How did the Christians suffer? Four trials are mentioned.**

● **Poverty**
*I know ... your poverty* (verse 9), Christ says. It is surprising that in wealthy and prosperous Smyrna any of its citizens should have been poor. Perhaps the Christians in Smyrna

belonged to the lower ranks of society, for we know that 'Not many ... were wise by human standards; not many were influential; not many were of noble birth' (1 Corinthians 1:26). Perhaps too the Christians' love for the underprivileged had led them to contribute so generously to their needs that they had impoverished themselves. But neither of these factors explains why their poverty was part of their *affliction.*

It seems probable that in their resolve to go straight in business, Christians had renounced shady methods and had thereby missed some of the easy profits which went to others less scrupulous than themselves. Or again, Jews and pagans may have been unwilling to trade with them. It may not have been easy for them to find employment. It is even possible that some of the Smyrna Christians had had their homes pillaged. To them it might have been written: 'You ... joyfully accepted the confiscation of your property, because you knew that you yourselves had better and lasting possessions' (Hebrews 10:34). Still today it does not always pay to be a Christian. Nor is honesty by any means always the best policy, if material gain is our ambition. Poverty has often been part of the cost of Christian discipleship.

### • Slander

*I know the slander of those who say they are Jews and are not* (verse 9). Jewish people were spreading false rumours about the Christians. Minds were being poisoned. Truly nobody can tame the tongue; it is a deadly evil (James 3:8). And slander is never easy to bear. The enemies of Christ were misrepresenting his people, 'blaspheming' them (for that is what the Greek word means). Christ calls them a *synagogue* not of the Lord but of *Satan* (verse 9, compare 3:9). For they had learned their ways from their master who is later called *the devil* (verse 10), which means 'the accuser', 'the slanderer'. Jesus had called him 'a liar and the father of lies' (John 8:44), and his followers share his distaste for the truth.

Gossip has a strange fascination for all of us. As the Book of Proverbs says: 'The words of a gossip are like choice morsels; they go down to a man's inmost parts' (Proverbs 26:22). And the unbelievers of Smyrna fully indulged their hunger for these succulent dainties. But the Christians were deeply wounded by their abuse. It was painful to be misunderstood and caricatured. Still, I do not doubt that they followed in the steps of their lowly Master, of whom it is written: 'When they hurled their insults at him, he did not retaliate; when he suffered, he made no threats. Instead, he entrusted himself to him who judges justly' (1 Peter 2:23).

Poverty and slander were the two experiences of affliction

which the church of Smyrna was already enduring. But there was more and worse to come. To this Christ now refers: *Do not be afraid of what you are about to suffer* (verse 10).

● **Prison**

*I tell you, the devil will put some of you in prison.* The early apostles, and the apostle Paul, had seen the inside of many prisons. The cells of Jerusalem and Caesarea, of Philippi and Rome, had been sanctified by their prayers and praises, and their prison darkness illumined by Christ's presence. It was in Neuchâtel prison in Switzerland that the daughter of William Booth, founder of the Salvation Army, wrote one of her well-known hymns:

> *Best-beloved of my soul,*
> *I am here alone with thee;*
> *And my prison is a heaven*
> *Since thou sharest it with me.*

● **Death**

*Be faithful, even to the point of death* (verse 10). Christ's exhortation to these persecuted believers was to be faithful 'to the extent of being ready to die for my sake' (Swete). Opposition to the gospel was so fierce that martyrdom appeared to be a real possibility. Indeed, one of the best-known Christian martyrs of all ages was a native of Smyrna. Reference has already been made to him earlier in this chapter. Polycarp was in all probability already a member of the church of Smyrna at the time the Revelation was written. Some have even argued that he was its chief minister, since both Tertullian and Irenaeus say that he was consecrated Bishop of Smyrna by John himself. At all events, he will have read this letter and no doubt pondered its message. Perhaps it was a source of strength to him when his hour of trial came. This is what happened.

**The death of Polycarp**

It was 2 February, probably in the year AD 156. The venerable bishop, who had fled from the city at the pleading of his congregation, was tracked down to his hiding-place. He made no attempt to flee. Instead he offered food and drink to his captors and asked permission to retire for prayer, which he did for two hours.

Then, as they travelled into the city, the officer in charge urged him to recant. 'What harm can it do,' he asked, 'to sacrifice to the emperor?' Polycarp refused. On arrival, he was roughly pushed out of the carriage, and brought before the proconsul in the amphitheatre, who addressed him: 'Respect

**Reliefs on an ancient sarcophagus, made to contain the body of a rich person.**

your years!... Swear by the genius of Caesar ...' And again, 'Swear, and I will release you; revile Christ!' To which Polycarp replied: 'For eighty-six years I have served him, and he has done me no wrong; how then can I blaspheme my king who saved me?' The proconsul persisted: 'Swear by the genius of Caesar.... I have wild beasts; if you will not change your mind, I will throw you to them ...' 'Call them,' Polycarp replied. 'Since you make light of the beasts, I will have you destroyed by fire, unless you change your attitude.'

Angry Jews and Gentiles then gathered wood for the pile. Polycarp stood by the stake, asking not to be fastened to it, and prayed 'O Lord, Almighty God, the Father of your beloved Son Jesus Christ, through whom we have come to know you ... I thank you for counting me worthy this day and hour of sharing the cup of Christ among the number of your martyrs.' The fire was lit, but as the wind drove the flames away from him and prolonged his suffering, a soldier put an end to his misery with a sword.

### A call to suffer

This call to suffer, here addressed to the church of Smyrna, is timeless in its application. According to the New Testament,

33

suffering is an indispensable mark of every true Christian and church, and the inevitability of persecution is repeatedly stressed. Jesus' final beatitude in the Sermon on the Mount reads: 'Blessed are you when people insult you, persecute you and falsely say all kinds of evil against you because of me. Rejoice and be glad, because great is your reward in heaven, for in the same way they persecuted the prophets who were before you.'

To this beatitude Jesus appended a complementary woe: 'Woe to you when all men speak well of you, for that is how their fathers treated the false prophets' (Matthew 5:10–12; Luke 6:26). Not once but many times this theme recurred in his teaching. 'If the world hates you, keep in mind that it hated me first... Remember the words I spoke to you: "No servant is greater than his master." If they persecuted me, they will persecute you also.' 'In this world you will have trouble' (John 15:18,20; 16:33). Jesus himself experienced the very same poverty and slander, arrest and death, of which he now writes to the church of Smyrna.

### Hallmark of the church

What Jesus taught, the apostles both echoed in their writings and endured in their ministries. The catalogue of Paul's sufferings makes lesser mortals tremble. He was imprisoned, flogged and shipwrecked; he braved the dangers of travel by sea, river and land, and was exposed to the savagery of innumerable enemies (2 Corinthians 11:23–27). No wonder he could write to Timothy: '...everyone who wants to live a godly life in Christ Jesus will be persecuted' (2 Timothy 3:12), and to the Philippians: '...it has been granted to you on behalf of Christ not only to believe on him, but also to suffer for him' (Philippians 1:29). Faith and suffering are thus linked together as twin Christian privileges.

Recent Christian writers have also recognized that suffering is the hallmark of the genuine church. Dietrich Bonhoeffer, the Lutheran pastor who was hanged by direct order of Himmler in the Flossenburg concentration camp in Germany on 9 April 1945, wrote: 'Suffering then is the badge of the true Christian. The disciple is not above his master.... Luther reckoned suffering among the marks of the true church.... Discipleship means allegiance to the suffering Christ, and it is therefore not at all surprising that Christians should be called upon to suffer ...' (*The Cost of Discipleship*).

Down the Christian centuries this has proved to be true, until in our own day in places like the Soviet Union, China, Uganda and South Africa, Christian people have suffered, or are suffering, for their faith.

### Compromise

What about ourselves? We are people of flesh. We shrink from suffering. The ugly truth is that we tend to avoid suffering by compromise.

Nothing provokes the world's opposition more than the gospel of Jesus Christ. For it emphasizes such unpalatable doctrines as the gravity of human sin and guilt, the reality of God's wrath and judgment, the impossibility of self-salvation, the necessity of the cross, the freeness of eternal life, and the dangers of eternal death. These truths undermine human pride and arouse human opposition. So preachers are tempted to mute them, in order 'to avoid being persecuted for the cross of Christ' (Galatians 6:12).

Christ's moral standards are also unpopular – honesty in business, chastity before marriage and fidelity after it, contentment in place of covetousness, self-control and self-sacrifice. If the church were to maintain such standards, it would find itself where it really belongs – outside the gate and in the wilderness. But the fear of the world has ensnared us. Our tendency is to dilute the gospel and to lower our standards in order not to give offence. We love the praise of our fellow human beings more than the praise of God.

I am not recommending that we develop a martyr-complex or that we court opposition. I am just saying that if we compromised less, we would undoubtedly suffer more. Smyrna was a suffering church because it was an uncompromising church.

It is good to note that the letter which Christ addressed to Smyrna was not just a stern warning of opposition. With the call to suffer there went the promise of accompanying grace. If Christ seldom makes offers without demands, he also seldom makes demands without offers. He offers his strength to enable us to meet his demands. So this letter, which is full of sufferings, is full of comforts and consolations too.

## The comforts they received from Christ

Christ's words of command are clear. *Do not be afraid of what you are about to suffer* and *Be faithful, even to the point of death* (verse 10). Here was an appeal to be faithful and not to be afraid. Faith and fear are opposites. They cannot co-exist. Faith banishes fear. 'When I am afraid,' wrote the Psalmist, 'I will trust in you' (Psalm 56:3). There is no other course to take. Jesus prescribed the same remedy. 'Do not be afraid,' he used to say, 'just believe' (Mark 5:36). True, here the call is to faithfulness rather than to faith, but we need to remember that faith and faithfulness are the same word in Greek. This is because it is from faith that faithfulness springs. Trust in Christ, and we shall ourselves be trustworthy. Rely on Christ, and we shall be reliable. Depend on Christ, and we shall be dependable. Have faith in Christ, and we shall be faithful – faithful if necessary even to the point of death. The way to lose fear is to gain faith.

But is Christ worthy of our trust when we suffer? In time of affliction our faith falters. How then can our trust in him grow so that, whether in light or in darkness, in sunshine or in storm, we shall put our whole confidence in him? The answer is that he is worthy of our implicit faith because of who and what he is. So he reveals here seven truths about himself, so that our trust in him may ripen and mature.

### • He is eternal

He is *the First and the Last* (verse 8). He has already thus described himself in the first chapter (verse 17), and has attached to this declaration a command not to be afraid. His word to John was 'Do not be afraid. I am the First and the Last.' It is an echo of what the Lord God had said in chapter 1 verse 8: 'I am the Alpha and the Omega'. Jesus now quietly assumes this divine title. He shares the eternal being of God. He is the beginning and the end, from everlasting to everlasting. In the midst of change he is unchanging. He is 'without beginning of days or end of life', 'the same yesterday and today and for ever' (Hebrews 7:3; 13:8). Before we were born he was Alpha, and he will be Omega after we have died. When fears grip the human heart, and our very life is threatened, nothing can bring tranquillity like faith in him who is both the first and the last.

### • He is victorious

He *died and came to life again* (verse 8). We live and die. Christ died and lived! Does he appeal to us to *be faithful, even to the point of death*? It is because he himself 'became obedient to death – even death on a cross' (Philippians 2:8). Death, even violent death, should hold no terrors for us if we believe that Jesus not only experienced it but actually conquered it. For about thirty-six hours he was held in the grip of death. But then on the third day he broke free from death's prison and emerged its triumphant victor. Now he is 'the Living One', who can say 'I was dead, and behold I am alive for ever and ever!' 'The keys of death and Hades' are in his hand (Revelation 1:18). He has roundly defeated him who had the power of death, that is the devil, so that he might free us from all fear of death (Hebrews 2:14,15).

The ancient marketplace of Smyrna, surrounded by the homes and offices of modern Smyrna.

### ● He is all-knowing

He says *I know your afflictions* (verse 9). This fact is the source of much comfort. One of our greatest needs in trouble is someone with whom to share it. We long to unburden ourselves to somebody who understands. Now Jesus Christ is the world's greatest confidant. No friend or father confessor can bring to us the peace and the relief that he can bring. We can then sing with the old plantation slaves:

*Nobody knows the trouble I've seen;*
*Nobody knows but Jesus.*

He knows because he walks among the lampstands. His knowledge is not a distant acquaintance with our circumstances; it is a close, personal understanding of us as people. His presence is never withdrawn. However deep our sorrow or great our suffering, he knows and cares.

### ● He is balanced

That is, he has a right sense of proportion and a true perspective. He says: *I know ... your poverty – yet you are rich!* His set of values is different from the world's. He looks not only on our material, but also on our spiritual, condition. Of course he cares deeply about the poor, the needy and the oppressed. Scripture makes that plain. At the same time, it adds that those who lack much of this world's goods can still be 'rich towards God', 'rich in faith', 'rich in good deeds', and have 'treasures in heaven' (Luke 12:21; James 2:5; 1 Timothy 6:18; Matthew 6:19,20 and 19:21).

It is possible to be impoverished in material things and yet enriched in Christ in every way, enjoying 'the unsearchable riches of Christ' (1 Corinthians 1:4; Ephesians 3:8). 'Though he was rich, yet for your sakes he became poor, so that you through his poverty might become rich' (2 Corinthians 8:9). The paradox is at its most dramatic in Paul's affirmation that he and his co-labourers were 'poor, yet making many rich; having nothing, and yet possessing everything' (2 Corinthians 6:10).

How do we measure wealth? In Archbishop Trench's words, there are in God's sight 'both poor rich-men and rich poor-men'. If we must choose, it is better to be described by Christ as 'poor yet rich' than to receive his condemnation of the rich Laodicean church as 'wretched, pitiful, poor, blind and naked' (chapter 3:17).

There was also another group in Smyrna who had a false perception of themselves: They *say they are Jews and are not, but are a synagogue of Satan* (verse 9). Their claim to be Jews was not accurate, because 'a man is not a Jew if he is only one outwardly ... a man is a Jew if he is one inwardly' (Romans 2:28,29). Thus, they say they are Jews, but they are not. And they say you are poor, but you are not. Both these judgments were mistaken. So we should not be too greatly concerned by the opinions of unbelievers, but rather cultivate the mind of Christ. Only he can see straight; all others are to some degree cross-eyed and squint.

### • He is in control

No suffering can engulf us except with his express permission. He has perfect knowledge of our present trials and perfect foreknowledge of our future afflictions. So, even while he warns the Christians of Smyrna about what is to come, he sets a limit to their sufferings. *I tell you, the devil will put some of you in prison to test you, and you will suffer persecution for ten days* (verse 10). Only some of you will be imprisoned, and the persecution will last only *for ten days* (a short, unspecified but restricted period). So a limit is set both to the number of Christians who will have to suffer this ordeal and to its duration.

**A Turkish cobbler at work.**

Those who know that God is on the throne and is in control of human affairs can remain calm amid the evils and sorrows of the world. As with the terrible afflictions of Job, and as with the mighty heathen empires which invaded Judah, God would say to the devil in Smyrna 'this far and no further'.

### • He is purposeful

The devil's consignment of certain Christians of Smyrna to prison was *to test you* (verse 10). This was Satan's self-confessed design. He was seeking to sift those believers as wheat is sifted when it is winnowed (compare Luke 22:31). He wanted the chaff to be blown away by the wind. But what Satan proposes, God permits. For God too has a purpose in suffering, and although the details of his purpose are often obscure, his general intention is clear. Our adversary tempts in order to destroy; our Father tests in order to refine. As gold is purified of dross in the furnace, so the fires of persecution can purge our Christian faith and strengthen our Christian character (James 1:2–4; 1 Peter 1:7). We need then to look beyond the trial to the purpose, beyond the pain of the chastening to its profit.

- **He is generous**

He promises a rich reward to the Christian who is steadfast through suffering. *Be faithful, even to the point of death, and I will give you the crown of life.... He who overcomes will not be hurt at all by the second death* (verses 10,11). We have already seen that each letter ends with the promise of an appropriate reward. *I will give,* Christ says. It is not a merit award; it is a gift. But he is generous in his gifts. If we endure, he says, and by our endurance prove the genuineness of our Christian profession, we shall escape the hell which is *the second death* (verse 11) and enter the heaven which is *the crown of life* (verse 10). We may need to be *faithful to the point of death,* but then *the second death* will not claim us. We may lose our life, but then *the crown of life* will be given us.

*The crown of life* (verse 10) is the same as *the tree of life* (verse 7), but the metaphor has changed. Heaven is now no longer a pleasure-garden, with eternal life as a tree bearing delicious fruit, but the winning-post at the end of a race, with eternal life as the victor's wreath or garland. Smyrna was famous for its arena and its games. So the Smyrna church will not have found it difficult to imagine the Christian life as a race or contest. It required diligent training, energy and strong exertion. The pace would be fast and the going hard. There would be sweat and pain. But at the end stood the One who is the first and the last, the supreme Victor; and in his hand was the crown of life which every conqueror would receive.

The message of the letter to the church of Smyrna is as searching for us as it was for them: if we are true, we shall suffer. But let us be faithful and not fear. Jesus Christ, the first and the last, who died and lives again, knows our trials, controls our destiny, and will invest us at the end of the race with the crown of life.

*'You remain true to my name. You did
not renounce your faith in me ...'*
Revelation 2:13

## The Letter to Pergamum:

# Truth

Revelation 2:12–17

Christ begins his letter to the church at Pergamum with the
statement *I know where you live* (verse 13). His knowledge of
the churches depends on his presence among them. He knows

**Inset: The massive Red
Basilica, Pergamum
(modern Bergama),
originally a temple to the
Egyptian god Serapis,
later a Christian basilica.**

them because he walks among them. Indeed, his intimate
knowledge of them extends beyond their works (as in Ephesus)
and their tribulation (as in Smyrna) to the environment in
which they live. *I know where you live* he says. He is aware that
his people are surrounded by a non-Christian society, and are

## Revelation 2:12–17

'To the angel of the church in Pergamum
write:

These are the words of him who has the
sharp, double-edged sword. ¹³I know where
you live – where Satan has his throne. Yet
you remain true to my name. You did not
renounce your faith in me, even in the days
of Antipas, my faithful witness, who was
put to death in your city – where Satan lives.
¹⁴Nevertheless, I have a few things against
you: You have people there who hold to the
teaching of Balaam, who taught Balak to
entice the Israelites to sin by eating food
sacrificed to idols and by committing sexual
immorality. ¹⁵Likewise you also have those
who hold to the teaching of the Nicolaitans.
¹⁶Repent therefore! Otherwise, I will soon
come to you and will fight against them with
the sword of my mouth.
¹⁷He who has an ear, let him hear what the
Spirit says to the churches. To him who
overcomes, I will give some of the hidden
manna. I will also give him a white stone
with a new name written on it, known only
to him who receives it.

exposed on all sides to the pressure of the world's standards and values. Their little boat is tossed about by the winds and waves of strange doctrines. Their fortress is bombarded by the gunfire of alien cults. They feel besieged, beleaguered.

### Pergamum

In no place was this more true than in Pergamum, which has been described as 'a strong centre of paganism'. Here a pitched battle was being fought, in which the combatants were not people but ideas. The issue was not between good and evil, but between truth and error.

Pergamum was about fifty-five miles from Smyrna, and as due north of it as Smyrna was of Ephesus. But it was some fifteen miles from the Aegean coast, and a mile or two from the River Caicus, in whose valley it was situated. No traveller could visit Pergamum without being impressed by its welter of temples and altars. 'The acropolis of Pergamum crowned a steep hill that rose one thousand feet above the plain. Near the summit stood an immense altar to Zeus, erected by Eumenes II to commemorate the victory won by his father over the Gauls; and at a short distance from this altar there was an elegant temple of Athena' (*Westminster Dictionary of the Bible*).

Other deities honoured in Pergamum were Dionysos and particularly Asklepios or Aesculapius, the 'saviour God' or god of healing, the remains of whose magnificent temple outside the city still remain. According to the classical historians Tacitus and Xenophon, the worship of Aesculapius had its headquarters in Pergamum, which thus became 'the Lourdes of the Province of Asia, and the seat of a famous school of medicine' (R.H.Charles).

### The imperial cult

More important still was the well-developed cult of Rome and Caesar which seems to have thrived in Pergamum. Back in 29 BC permission had been granted to the citizens of Pergamum to erect and dedicate a temple to Augustus. This was the first provincial temple to be built in honour of a living emperor. Smyrna's came three years later in 26 BC. 'The imperial cult had thus its centre at Pergamum' (R.H.Charles).

It appears from this prevalence of religious superstition that antichrist was more evident in Pergamum than Christ. What had Christ to say to a church oppressed by such influences?

## Christ's concern for the truth

The exalted Christ is deeply concerned that the truth be both preserved and spread. This is the theme of the letter. He commends the church because, he says, *you remain true to my*

*name. You did not renounce your faith* (verse 13). But he adds a complaint that, although they had maintained their own theological convictions, they yet tolerated in their fellowship some false prophets. *I have a few things against you: You have people there who hold the teaching of Balaam* (verse 14). Instead of 'holding' Christ's name, they were 'holding' a false cult (the Greek verb is the same), and this was deeply disturbing to the church's Heavenly Overseer. The guarding of the truth of the gospel is a major concern of Jesus Christ. He is not only anxious that we should love him, and that we should suffer bravely for him, but also that we should believe in him and hold fast the truth about him.

**Love and truth**
It is striking that according to these letters love is the first mark of a true and living church and truth is the second, because the Scriptures hold love and truth together in balance. Some Christians are so resolved to make love paramount, that they forget the sacredness of revealed truth. 'Let us drown our doctrinal differences,' they urge, 'in the ocean of brotherly love!' Others are equally mistaken in their pursuit of truth at the expense of love. So dogged is their zeal for God's word that they become harsh, bitter and unloving. Love becomes sentimental if it is not strengthened by truth, and truth becomes hard if it is not softened by love. We need to preserve the balance of the Bible which tells us to hold the truth in love, to love others in the truth, and to grow not only in love but in discernment (Ephesians 4:15; 3 John 1; Philippians 1:9).

Let those who say that it does not matter what you believe so long as you live well and love all, read, mark, learn and inwardly digest this letter. Let them consider the attitude and gain the mind of our Lord Jesus Christ. He does not share the lack of doctrinal concern which is exhibited by such people. He called himself 'the truth' and 'the light of the world'. He promised his disciples that if they continued in his word they would know the truth and the truth would liberate them. He told Pontius Pilate that he had come into the world to bear witness to the truth (John 14:6; 8:12, 31–32; 18:37). So it is plain that he loves the truth, he speaks the truth, he is the truth. How then can his followers be indifferent to it?

At Pergamum it seems that most church members were continuing to walk in the truth. Only a few, whether in full fellowship or in casual association with the church, had departed from the narrow path of revelation and wandered into the byways of speculation and error. But the risen Christ, the Chief Shepherd of his flock, was grieved both by the waywardness of the minority and by the nonchalance of the majority. *You have*

The impressive Temple of Trajan, built on the Acropolis, Pergamum, for the worship of the Roman Emperor Trajan.

*people there who hold to the teaching of Balaam ... you also have those who hold to the teaching of the Nicolaitans* (verses 14, 15), he complains. Did they not care that the truth was being challenged, even eclipsed? Did it mean nothing to them that Christ's name was being dishonoured by some and his faith denied? *Repent therefore!* he cried (verse 16).

### Does truth matter?
But what is truth, as (in Francis Bacon's famous phrase) Pilate asked 'and would not stay for an answer'? Was the situation in Pergamum really as serious as Christ appears to suggest? I hope to show in the next chapter that the letters to Pergamum and Thyatira leave room for debate and disagreement on peripheral matters, while insisting that the central Christian truths cannot be compromised. How wise was Rupert Meldenius in the seventeenth century, who is quoted as saying that we must preserve unity in essentials, liberty in non-essentials and charity in all things. Many of our troubles in inter-church relations arise from our lack of proportion. We minimize the central and magnify the peripheral. We make concessions on clearly revealed truths which should never be surrendered, and

yet insist upon secondary matters and even on trivialities which are neither revealed nor required by God.

What then are these central truths? I believe they can be reduced to two, both of which are implicit in this letter to Pergamum.

### Truth about Christ

The first is a doctrinal truth concerning Christ. It has been rightly said that Christianity is Christ. Jesus Christ himself is the rock on which the structure of Christian theology is built. To be a Christian is to accept Jesus Christ as God and Saviour. The irreducible minimum of Christian belief is that Jesus of Nazareth is the unique God-man who died for our sins and was raised from death to be the Saviour of the world. We may not (in fact, we do not) fully understand these truths about the person and work of Jesus Christ, but Christians believe them and act on them. For conviction leads to commitment. If Jesus is *the* divine Lord, we must submit to him as *our* Lord. If he is *the* divine Saviour, we must trust in him as *our* Saviour. This personal appropriation of Jesus Christ is essential.

All this is implied in the two phrases by which the Lord Jesus describes the Christians of Pergamum. *You remain true to my name. You did not renounce your faith in me ...* (verse 13). What does he mean by these references to his name and their faith? His name stands for himself. It is the revelation of who he is and what he has done. It represents the fulness of his divine-human person and saving work. To *remain true* to his name is therefore to hold firmly to our conviction that he is both Lord and Saviour, and never let it go. The phrase *your faith in me* takes us a stage further. As we have seen, it is not enough to give intellectual assent to Christ's Lordship and Saviourhood; we must also put our trust in him as our personal Saviour and Lord. We must not only hold fast his name but exercise faith in him.

These fundamental truths cannot be compromised. The apostles make this abundantly clear in the New Testament. We cannot regard as Christians any who deny either the divine-human person of Jesus or his unique saving work. There is no room for negotiation or appeasement here. To deny that Jesus is 'the Christ come in the flesh' is antichrist, wrote John, while to preach any gospel other than the gospel of Christ's saving grace is to deserve Paul's anathema (1 John 2:22; 4:2; 2 John 7–11; Galatians 1:6–9).

### Antipas the martyr

The Pergamum Christians' grasp of these central truths had evidently been put to a severe test. They had been sorely tempted to give in. But they had stood firm. They had not followed the cowardly example of Peter who denied Jesus. They had not denied Christ's faith; they remained true to his name. Indeed, one of their number in the heat of the persecution had been faithful even to the point of death. We know nothing about him except what may be gathered here. His name was Antipas. His courage cost him his life, and Jesus accords to him his own title 'faithful witness' (1:5; 3:14) when he refers to him affectionately as *Antipas, my faithful witness, who was put to death in your city* (verse 13).

It is not hard to reconstruct the scene which probably saw the death of Antipas. Known to be a Christian, he was summoned before the proconsul of the province, whose official residence is thought by some to have been in Pergamum. This civil leader was also chief priest of the imperial cult. A bust of the emperor was set on a plinth and sacred fire burned before it. To sacrifice to the genius of Rome and the divine Emperor was a simple matter. All he had to do was to sprinkle a few grains of incense on the fire and say 'Caesar is Lord'. Then he would be released. But how could he deny Christ's name and faith? Had he not at his baptism been proud to affirm his faith, in the simple words 'Jesus is Lord'? Had he not been instructed that God had exalted Jesus to his own right hand and set him 'far above all rule and authority, power and dominion and every title that can be given', and given him 'the name that is above every name, that at the name of Jesus every knee should bow ... and every tongue confess that Jesus Christ is Lord to the glory of God the Father'? Had his teachers not assured him that to say 'Jesus is Lord' was a sign of the Holy Spirit's inspiration, whereas no one can say 'Jesus be cursed' when speaking by the Spirit of God (Ephesians 1:20, 21; Philippians 2:9–11; 1 Corinthians 12:3)?

Such thoughts as these must have invaded the mind of Antipas as his Christian faith was exposed to its supreme test. Whether he wavered or not, we cannot say. All we know is that he was given grace to stand firm, to hold fast Christ's name and not to deny Christ's faith. He would indeed render to Caesar the things that were Caesar's, but he must also render to God the things that were God's. He could not bring himself to give to Caesar the title that belonged to Christ. Christ was his Lord, not Caesar, even if it meant the whip, the sword, the stake or the lions. So Antipas joined 'the noble army of martyrs'. He was a faithful witness, and sealed his testimony with his blood.

### Truth about holiness

The second central truth which cannot at any price be sacrificed is an ethical one. It concerns holiness. The Christian faith is essentially concerned with the person and work of Christ on the one hand and the life of righteousness on the other. Christianity exalts Christ and promotes holiness. To deny Christ and to follow evil are to surrender the citadel of Christianity to the enemy and to haul down the standard of truth. The New Testament writers insist on the defence of these two bastions. They are as savage in their denunciation of immoral people as they are of those who forsake Christ and his gospel.

There is room for a difference of opinion about minor points of doctrine and ethics, but in these areas there must be unanimity and no compromise. John's first letter is devoted to this theme – that those who are born of God both believe in Christ and practise righteousness, both walk in the truth and walk in the light. To deny that Jesus is the Christ is to be a liar; to claim to know God and to disobey his commandments is to be a liar also. Similarly, Paul urges the Corinthians not to associate with any Christian brother if by choice and practice he is 'sexually immoral or greedy, an idolator or a slanderer, a drunkard or a swindler. With such a man do not even eat' (1 John 2:4, 22; 1 Corinthians 5:11).

## Nicolaitans and Balaamites

This vehement rejection of sin and this passionate love of righteousness emerge clearly in the letter to the church of Pergamum. The Pergamum Christians harboured in their midst some who held *the teaching of Balaam ... and the teaching of the Nicolaitans* (verses 14, 15). It is commonly agreed that the Balaamites and the Nicolaitans were the same teachers, and are not to be distinguished from each other. They were to be found also in the church of Ephesus. Why they were called *Nicolaitans* we have discussed in connection with the letter to that church. We must now enquire what their relation was to Balaam.

Balaam was that remarkable prophet whose story is told in chapters 22 to 24 of the book of Numbers. Balak, king of Moab, had summoned him to come and curse the tribes of Israel who were about to cross over the River Jordan into the Promised Land. But every time Balaam opened his mouth, the words the Lord gave him to speak were words not of cursing but of blessing. Moved (according to 2 Peter 2:15 and Jude 11) by greed for the reward Balak was offering him, Balaam then devised another scheme for the downfall of Israel. He suggested to Balak that Moabite girls should seduce the Israelite men, by inviting them to take part in their idolatrous and immoral feasts. He knew, and knew rightly, that this would provoke the righteous God of Israel to anger. So *Balaam ...*

**The Sacred Way, at the Asclepion of Pergamum, built to honour the god of healing, Asklepios.**

*taught Balak to entice the Israelites to sin by eating food sacrificed to idols and by committing sexual immorality* (verse 14; compare Numbers 25 and 31:16).

### Travesty of truth

What Balaam was to the old Israel, the Nicolaitans evidently were to the new. They were insinuating their vile doctrines into the church. They were daring to suggest that the liberty with which Christ has made us free was a liberty to sin. 'Christ has redeemed us from the law', they seem to have argued. 'Therefore we are no longer under law but under grace. And so,' their specious argument continued, 'we may continue in sin that God's grace may continue to abound towards us in forgiveness.' This travesty of the truth was to 'change the grace of our God into a licence for immorality and deny Jesus Christ our only Sovereign and Lord' (Galatians 5:1; Romans 6:1; Jude 4).

'Just a little idolatry,' they murmured. 'Just a little immorality. We are free. We do not have to go to extremes.' Such perverse reasoning is sometimes heard in the churches today. 'It is no use being idealistic,' it is said. 'We are all human, you know. Christ does not expect too much from us. His demands are not unreasonable. He knows we are dust.' Totally different is Christ's view of this matter. Some manuscripts conclude verse

15 (as in the King James Version) *...the teaching of the Nicolaitans, which I hate.* The words may not be original here, but they are true. Sin to Christ is 'that abominable thing which I hate'. The church of Ephesus hated 'the practices of Nicolaitans' (verse 6), and were commended for their holy hatred. Christ even adds in that letter 'I also hate' them. But what was hated in Ephesus was tolerated in Pergamum. So Christ calls the church to *repent* (verse 16), to repent of its error and its evil, for he is deeply concerned about a church which is tainted with such things.

## Christ's recognition of the source of error

We turn from a consideration of Christ's concern for the truth to note his recognition of the origin of error. It is diabolical. The church of Pergamum lived and worshipped and witnessed *where Satan lives* (verse 13b), *where Satan has his throne* (verse 13a). Satan not only inhabited Pergamum, but ruled it. The implication is clear, namely that Satan was the source of the errors to which some church members had succumbed.

We need to rid our minds of the medieval caricature of Satan. Dispensing with the horns, the hooves and the tail, we are left with the biblical portrait of a spiritual being, highly intelligent, immensely powerful and utterly unscrupulous. Jesus himself not only believed in his existence, but warned us of his power. He called him 'the prince of this world', much as Paul called him 'the ruler of the kingdom of the air'. He has therefore a throne and a kingdom, and under his command is an army of malignant spirits who are described in Scripture as 'the powers of this dark world', and 'the spiritual forces of evil in the heavenly realms' (John 12:31; Ephesians 2:2; 6:12).

### Satan's overthrow

But Satan and his forces have been overthrown. Christ saw Satan fall like lightning from heaven, and John later in the Revelation describes how the dragon and his angels, after being defeated by Michael and his angels, were 'hurled down'. At the cross Jesus met and conquered all the powers of evil. As they closed in upon him, he stripped them from him like a filthy garment, and 'made a public spectacle of them, triumphing over them by the cross'. There Satan's head was crushed, although in the doing of it Christ's heel was bruised (Luke 10:18; Revelation 12:7–12; Colossians 2:15; Genesis 3:15).

Despite their overthrow, the powers of darkness have not yet conceded their defeat; they continue to contest every inch of their territory. The kingdom of Satan retreats only as the kingdom of God advances. In some places he holds almost

undisputed sway. Pergamum was such a place. *I know where you live,* says Jesus to the church, *you live ... where Satan lives* (verse 13). Its multitudinous temples, shrines and altars, its labyrinth of antichristian philosophies, its grant of refuge to antinomian Nicolaitans and Balaamites, all bore eloquent testimony to the dominion of the evil one. Perhaps in mentioning Satan, who is *that ancient serpent* (Revelation 12:9), Christ is making a veiled allusion to the cult of Aesculapius, whose symbol was a serpent. Perhaps also Satan's *throne* refers to the massive altar to Zeus the Saviour 'which seemed to dominate the place from its platform cut in the Acropolis rock' (Swete).

But the chief menace of Satan lay in the claims of the imperial religion. It was through a refusal to take part in this that Antipas had lost his life. It was here that the dragon's authority was most clearly seen.

**The vaulting which supports the back tiers of the theatre, Pergamum.**

### A dark place

So Pergamum was a dark place. The light of truth filtered only weakly into it. It was steeped in the dense fogs of error. For Satan's realm is where 'darkness reigns'; he is the ruler of 'this dark world' and 'hates the light' (Luke 22:53; Ephesians 6:12; John 3:20). He is called in Scripture both a liar and a deceiver. He is said to blind the minds of unbelievers. He not only entices mortals into sin, but beguiles them into error (John 8:44; 2 Corinthians 4:4). Later in the Revelation we are introduced to the dragon's allies. One of them is a monster 'coming out of the earth', later called 'the false prophet'. Its function is to make 'the earth and its inhabitants worship the first beast' (Revelation 13:11, 12; 19:20). Since this 'first beast' rose out of the sea and was worshipped, it seems to stand for the persecuting Roman Empire, in which case the second beast will represent the emperor-cult.

The emperor-cult has long since vanished. But 'the false prophet' has not died. He lives again in every non-Christian religion and philosophy, and in every attempt to divert to others the honour that is due to Jesus Christ alone. This is the spirit of antichrist. This is the work of Satan.

# Christ's resolve that truth shall triumph over error

Concerned that his church shall stand in the truth, and recognizing the source of error, Jesus Christ is resolved that the truth shall triumph. He calls upon the church of Pergamum, which has permitted grievous error to be taught unchecked, both to *repent* (verse 16) and to gain the victory over falsehood. He then indicates both the way of conquest and its reward.

The way of conquest is by his word. The only weapon which can slay the forces of error is the word of Christ. No wonder, as he dictates this letter to John, he describes himself as he *who has the sharp, double-edged sword* (verse 12). In the vision of the exalted Christ which John saw and described in the first chapter of the Revelation, this sharp double-edged sword came from his mouth (Revelation 1:16), because it is a symbol of the word of truth which he has spoken. Indeed, he is himself 'the Word of God' (Revelation 19:13; compare John 1:1).

### The double-edged sword

The picture of Christ with a sword flashing from his mouth may seem to us very peculiar, but it is 'not so strange as appears at first sight, for the short Roman sword was tongue-like in shape' (Hastings' *Dictionary of the Bible*). Already in the prophecy of Isaiah the Servant of Yahweh (prefiguring Christ) says of himself: 'He made my mouth like a sharpened sword'

(Isaiah 49:2). The word of God is said by the apostle Paul to be 'the sword of the Spirit', and in the letter to the Hebrews to be 'living and active'. Indeed, 'Sharper than any double-edged sword, it penetrates even to dividing soul and spirit, joints and marrow; it judges the thoughts and attitudes of the heart' (Ephesians 6:17; Hebrews 4:12). Whether or not we agree with Tertullian and Augustine that the two edges of the sword represent the Old and New Testaments, the Bible has many sword-like qualities. It pricks the conscience, and wounds the pride of sinners. It cuts away our camouflage and pierces our defences. It lays bare our sin and need, and kills all false doctrine by its deft, sharp thrusts.

God's way to overcome error is the proclamation of the gospel of Christ, which is God's power for salvation to everyone who believes. Falsehood will not be suppressed by the gruesome methods of the inquisition, or by the burning of heretics at the stake, or by restrictive legislation. Ideas will not be overcome by force. Only truth can defeat error. The false ideologies of the world can be overthrown only by the superior ideology of Christ. We have no weapon other than this sword. We must use it fearlessly.

### Message of judgment
One day this same sword will change its function. The message of truth will become the message of judgment. The sword to pierce the conscience will be the sword to destroy the soul. *I will soon come to you and will fight against them with the sword of my mouth* (verse 16; compare Revelation 19:15,21). Balaam himself was killed with the sword (Numbers 31:8; Joshua 13:22), and the Balaamites in Pergamum (unless they repent) will suffer the same fate, except that now the sword will be the word of Christ. In other words the very gospel of Christ which saves those who obey it destroys those who disobey it.

If anything is certain about divine judgment in Scripture, it is that God will hold us responsible for our response to that measure of truth which we have known. And from those to whom much is revealed, much will be required. As Jesus said to his contemporaries: 'As for the person who hears my words but does not keep them, I do not judge him. For I did not come to judge the world, but to save it. There is a judge for the one who rejects me and does not accept my words; that very word which I spoke will condemn him at the last day' (John 12:47,48). Here is Christ's saving word turned judge, his wholesome sword turned executioner.

Having outlined God's weapon for the conquest of error, Christ now describes his reward to the conqueror – that is, to

**The sacred well, or fountain, in the Asclepion of Pergamum.**

the man or woman who hears and receives his word, seeks to understand it and strives to live by it. *To him who overcomes, I will give some of the hidden manna. I will also give him a white stone with a new name written on it, known only to him who receives it* (verse 17).

### Hidden manna

Here are two precious and desirable gifts, the hidden manna and a white stone inscribed with a new name. What do these presents mean? The hiddenness of the manna probably alludes to the 'gold jar of manna' which was kept in the ark (Exodus 16:32–34; Hebrews 9:4), but the manna itself is Christ. Just as God's people were fed by manna in the wilderness, so today our spiritual hunger is satisfied by Christ, the bread of life. He himself, after feeding the five thousand, claimed to be 'the true bread from heaven ...' which 'gives life to the world' (John 6:31–35) and 'the living bread that came down from heaven' so that 'if anyone eats of this bread, he will live for ever' (John 6:48–51). But the promised reward with which each of the seven letters closes is a reward to be inherited in heaven, not on earth. So the hidden manna must look beyond our present taste of Christ to the heavenly feast which awaits us. Denying

**Schoolgirls in the village street of Bergama, ancient Pergamum.**

ourselves the luxury of idol-meats in this life, the banquet will be the richer in the next.

### The white stone

As for the white stone inscribed with the new name, commentators have tumbled over one another with the variety of their interpretations. Some refer us to the jewels which, according to Rabbinical tradition, fell from the sky with the manna. Others write of the white ballot pebble which was thrown into a box by the judge when he acquitted a prisoner, while yet others remind us of the *tessara* given to winners in the games, entitling them to free access to the public entertainments. Stones were used as amulets, as counters and as tickets, and all these have been suggested for consideration here.

But to me Archbishop Trench's explanation is the most reasonable. He recalls how the mysterious 'Urim and Thummim', mentioned many times in the Old Testament, were consulted by the High Priest when he was seeking divine guidance. They were connected with the twelve precious stones, symbolizing the twelve tribes of Israel, which were set in the High Priest's breastplate. The Urim, Trench thought, may have been a 'white stone' or diamond on which was written, it has often been conjectured, the secret name of God. Since the pot of manna was hidden within the veil (which was entered only by the High Priest), and since Urim was possessed and consulted by the High Priest only, Trench suggested that both the manna and the stone to be presented to the Christian conqueror represent the privileges of the high priest, which the Lord will ultimately bestow on all his people, whom he has made his priests (Revelation 1:6; 5:10).

### The new name

Whatever the stone may be, the new name to be engraved on it is undoubtedly the name of Christ, who says later in his letter to the Philadelphian church: 'I will also write on him my new name' (Revelation 3:12). The name is secret, just as the manna is hidden, for it will be disclosed only to him who receives it. What will be written on the white stone will be *a new name ... known only to him who receives it* (verse 17). The intimate self-revelation promised by Christ to the believer in paradise will be private and personal. Heaven will indeed be a community, but that does not mean that we shall be like a herd of indistinguishable cattle. We shall retain our individuality and our personal relationship to Christ.

*Write your new name upon my heart*
*Your new, best name of love.*

What then is the promise of the manna and the name on the stone? It is the pledge of a fuller revelation to those who hold fast the revelation already granted. The hidden manna is Christ. The new name is Christ. We shall feast on the manna and comprehend the name. This is the beatific vision. It will be to receive such a manifestation of Christ as shall completely satisfy both heart and mind. Those who hold fast Christ's name shall receive a deeper revelation of it, *a new name*. Those who do not deny Christ's faith will be satisfied by the hidden manna. Those who know in part shall know also as they are known. Those who see Christ now in a mirror dimly shall see him face to face.

So, recognizing Christ's concern for the triumph of his truth, and Satan's activity in the spread of lies, we are called to guard what has been entrusted to us and 'contend for the faith that was once for all entrusted to the saints' (1 Timothy 6:20; Jude 3). And we are to hold this truth in love.

*'I have this against you: You tolerate
that woman Jezebel ...'*
Revelation 2:20

## The Letter to Thyatira:

# Holiness

Revelation 2:18–29

'The longest letter is addressed to the least important of the Seven Cities' (R.H.Charles). The city of Thyatira was certainly smaller and less significant than the previous three. It was situated about half-way between Pergamum and Sardis on the great circular road of the province of Asia which has been mentioned previously. The postman entrusted with delivering these letters, having begun his round at Ephesus, and having travelled due north from there to Smyrna and further north to Pergamum, will have had then to turn south-east and journey forty miles in order to reach Thyatira.

**Thyatira**
If Thyatira was noted for anything, it had a commercial rather than a political distinction. It was evidently at that time a pros-

---

### Revelation 2:18–29

'To the angel of the church in Thyatira write:

These are the words of the Son of God, whose eyes are like blazing fire and whose feet are like burnished bronze. [19]I know your deeds, your love and faith, your service and perseverance, and that you are now doing more than you did at first.
[20]Nevertheless, I have this against you: You tolerate that woman Jezebel, who calls herself a prophetess. By her teaching she misleads my servants into sexual immorality and the eating of food sacrificed to idols. [21]I have given her time to repent of her immorality, but she is unwilling. [22]So I will cast her on a bed of suffering, and I will make those who commit adultery with her suffer intensely, unless they repent of her

ways. [23]I will strike her children dead. Then all the churches will know that I am he who searches hearts and minds, and I will repay each of you according to your deeds. [24]Now I say to the rest of you in Thyatira, to you who do not hold to her teaching and have not learned Satan's so-called deep secrets (I will not impose any other burden on you): [25]Only hold on to what you have until I come.
[26]To him who overcomes and does my will to the end, I will give authority over the nations –
[27]'He will rule them with an iron sceptre;
  he will dash them to pieces like pottery'–
just as I have received authority from my Father. [28]I will also give him the morning star. [29]He who has an ear, let him hear what the Spirit says to the churches.

**An ancient tombstone or stela.**

perous trading centre. Inscriptions which archaeologists have brought to light reveal the interesting fact that Thyatira boasted numerous trade guilds. There were, for example, associations for bakers and bronze-workers, for clothiers and cobblers, for weavers, tanners, dyers and potters. It was from Thyatira that Lydia, one of Philippi's most notable converts, had come. She traded in materials treated with Thyatira's purple dye and is described by Luke as 'a dealer in purple cloth' (Acts 16:14). She had evidently emigrated (presumably on business) to Philippi in Macedonia, of which Thyatira was a colony, and there she heard Paul preach the gospel. The Lord opened her heart to listen to the message. She believed and was baptized.

Perhaps it was Lydia, newborn in Christ, who returned to her home in Thyatira and was the means of planting the Christian church there. We do not know. Certainly by the time the Revelation was written, this prosperous city had a prosperous church. Jesus Christ speaks of it in words of warmest commendation. *I know your deeds,* he writes, *your love and faith, your service and perseverance* (verse 19). Here are four sterling Christian qualities indeed. Thyatira not only rivalled Ephesus in busy Christian service, but exhibited the love which Ephesus lacked, preserved the faith which was imperilled at Pergamum, and shared with Smyrna the virtue of patient endurance in tribulation.

### A beautiful garden

Indeed, Thyatira's church was like a beautiful garden in which the fairest Christian graces blossomed; both a humble ministry on the one hand, and on the other that trinity so often described by Paul: faith, hope and love. Faith and love are mentioned by name, and what is *perseverance* but the fruit of hope? We are reminded forcibly of Paul's commendation of the Thessalonian believers 'We continually remember before our God and Father your work produced by faith, your labour prompted by love, and your endurance inspired by hope in our Lord Jesus Christ' (1 Thessalonians 1:3). Here too at Thyatira there was a practical love resulting in service, together with a virile faith and hope tending to endurance.

But Thyatira's catalogue of virtues is not exhausted yet. *I know your deeds,* Christ says, and adds: *and that you are now doing more than you did at first* (verse 19). The church of Thyatira understood that the Christian life is a life of growth, of progress, of development. Ephesus was backsliding; Thyatira was moving forward. The church of Ephesus had abandoned the love it had at first; the church of Thyatira was exceeding the works it did at first.

## Christian growth

Christian growth is variously illustrated in the New Testament. Now it is like the gradual maturing of a human being, from infancy through adolescence to adult stature; now it is the increasing fruitfulness of a vine; and now the chemical process employed for refining metals. All these similes imply a movement which is steady but sure, positive and purposive.

Is our Christian life like that? We began well, no doubt. But how are we faring now? Are we standing still, or falling back, or going on? The New Testament speaks of a growth in faith and love, in knowledge and holiness. Paul could rejoice, when writing a second letter to the Thessalonians, 'because your faith is growing more and more, and the love every one of you has for each other is increasing' (2 Thessalonians 1:3). The Christians of Thyatira were also growing – growing in *love and faith ... service and perseverance* (verse 19).

## A poisonous weed

In view of this church's splendid record, it is sad to read a little further and discover its moral compromise. In that fair field a poisonous weed was being allowed to luxuriate. In that healthy body a malignant cancer had begun to form. An enemy was being harboured in the midst of the fellowship. *I have this against you,* the letter continues, *You tolerate that woman Jezebel, who calls herself a prophetess. By her teaching she misleads my servants into sexual immorality and the eating of food sacrificed to idols* (verse 20). The church of Thyatira displayed love and faith, service and endurance, but holiness is not included among its qualities. It permitted one of its female members to teach outrageous licence, and it apparently made no attempt to restrain her. In this too the church of Thyatira was the opposite of the church of Ephesus. Ephesus could not bear evil, self-styled apostles, but had no love (Revelation 2:2, 4). Thyatira had love, but tolerated an evil, self-styled prophetess.

## Christian holiness

Holiness of life and character is, then, another indispensable mark of the real Christian and of the true church. It is much emphasized in the New Testament. 'It is God's will that you should be sanctified: that you should avoid sexual immorality'. Holiness is not only God's will, but his purpose. It is the purpose of the Father's election: 'He chose us in him (that is, Christ) before the creation of the world to be holy and blameless in his sight'. It is the purpose of the Son's death: 'Jesus Christ ... gave himself for us to redeem us from all wickedness and to purify for himself a people that are his very own, eager

to do what is good'. It is the purpose of the Holy Spirit's indwelling: 'God did not call us to be impure, but to live a holy life ... who gives you his Holy Spirit' (1 Thessalonians 4:3; Ephesians 1:4; Titus 2:13, 14; 1 Thessalonians 4:7,8). Here then are the Father, the Son and the Holy Spirit, the three Persons of the one eternal Godhead, united in their purpose to make us holy.

But if it is God's purpose to make us holy, Satan is resolved to frustrate it. He is seeking ceaselessly to entice both believers and churches into sin. If the monster from the sea fails to crush the church by force, and the monster from the earth to pervert its testimony by error, then the Babylonian harlot may succeed in seducing it by her loathsome charms (compare Revelation 17:1–6). Or, to drop the vivid imagery of the Revelation, if the devil cannot destroy the church by persecution or heresy, he will try to corrupt it with evil. Such at least was the dragon's strategy in Thyatira.

### Jezebel

But who was *that woman Jezebel*? There is no need to go to the extremes of supposing either that there was a real woman of that name in Thyatira or that the expression merely represents an evil influence. She was a real woman alright, but the name is surely as symbolical as other Old Testament names in this book, such as Balaam, Sodom, Babylon and Jerusalem? What is meant is that this disreputable prophetess was as wicked and dangerous an influence in Thyatira as Jezebel had been in Israel.

Queen Jezebel was the wife of that weak king, Ahab. She was a foreigner and had imported into Israel her alien cult. Her father, Ethbaal, was a priest of Astarte who had succeeded to the throne of Sidon by murdering his predecessor. Astarte, or Ashtaroth, was the Phoenician equivalent of the Greek goddess Aphrodite and the Roman Venus. Her beastly system had engineered such a complete divorce of morality from religion that it even encouraged gross sexual immorality under the cloak of piety. According to one etymology 'Jezebel' means 'pure' or 'chaste'; but Jezebel contradicted her name by her character and her behaviour.

When Jezebel married King Ahab, she became active in the diffusion of her revolting doctrines in Israel. She may even have been a priestess of Astarte herself. She persuaded Ahab to build a temple and altar to Astarte in his capital, Samaria. She supported 850 prophets of her immoral cult and killed off all the prophets of righteous Yahweh on whom she could lay her hands. She became well-known for what Jehu later called her 'idolatry and witchcraft' (1 Kings 16:30–32; 18:4, 19; 21:25;

**Fallen columns at Akhisar, ancient Thyatira.**

2 Kings 9:22). She sought to contaminate Israel, as Balaam had done before her, and Ahab lacked the moral conviction or stamina to withstand her.

### The second Jezebel

The first Jezebel had now been dead nearly a thousand years. She had met a horrible end. But her evil spirit had, as it were, become reincarnate in a prophetess of the first century AD, whose religion had as little connection with morality as that of her namesake. Laying claim to divine inspiration, she was succeeding in persuading the servants of Christ to indulge in immoral practices. R.H.Charles thought that she was encouraging the Christians of Thyatira to attend the ceremonies and feasts of the local trade-guilds which were 'dedicated no doubt to some pagan deity' and 'too often ended in unbridled licentiousness'.

The new Jezebel and her followers probably prided themselves on their mature experience of life. Like the later Gnostics, they were delving into secret mysteries and boasting of a private, esoteric revelation denied to the mass of Christians. They saw themselves as a spiritual aristocracy, a favoured elite. They bragged that they plumbed 'the deep things'. Perhaps they even borrowed this phrase from Paul, who mentioned several times in his letters 'the deep things of God' – the

63

deeps of his wisdom and love which human beings can know only because the Holy Spirit explores and reveals them (Romans 11:33; Ephesians 3:18; 1 Corinthians 2:10). If the Gnostics borrowed the phrase from Paul, they then perverted it. With their diabolical theory that since matter was evil the sins of the flesh could be freely indulged without damage to the spirit, they plunged without restraint into *Satan's so-called deep secrets* (verse 24).

**Tolerating sin**

It seems, then, that the Jezebelites were similar to, if not identical with, the Nicolaitans and the Balaamites. Their practices of *sexual immorality* and *eating of food sacrificed to idols* (verse 20) are both mentioned in this letter to Thyatira as they have been in the earlier letter to Pergamum (verse 14). Here, however, the emphasis seems to be on their sin rather than on their error, on a question of ethics rather than of doctrine. The church was allowing Jezebel and her brood to continue unchecked. Ephesus 'hated' the practices of the Nicolaitans and could not tolerate them (verse 2, 6); Pergamum had some who held the teaching of Balaam and of the Nicolaitans (verses 14, 15); but Thyatira actually *tolerated* them (verse 20). The Christians of Thyatira seem to have had either a very poor conscience or a very feeble courage. They were as weak and spineless towards the new Jezebel as Ahab had been towards the old. Christ complained that she had contrived to deceive his servants into sin. It is as if he said: '*My servants* (verse 20) are committed to obey me not Jezebel. To serve her is the licence which is slavery; to follow me is the service which is freedom.'

What message has the ascended Christ to a church in this condition?

# Christ's statement to the whole church

He begins his message to the Thyatira church, as he begins the other letters, by saying: *I know,* but somehow in this letter the words have a more forceful meaning. All the churches needed to understand that he was their heavenly supervisor, who was walking among the lampstands, but Thyatira needed this assurance more than the rest, because many of the vile practices of the Jezebel party were being indulged in secret. Perhaps the church itself did not fully know what was going on behind locked doors and in the darkness. But Christ knew. He had good reason to introduce himself to this church as *the Son of God, whose eyes are like blazing fire* (verse 18; compare Revelation 1:14; 19:12). They pierced the night which shrouded Jezebel's sins, and flashed with fiery indignation.

## Burning eyes

The eyes of Jesus must have fascinated people when he was on earth. The Pharisees seemed to shrivel up in shame when 'he looked round at them in anger ... deeply distressed at their stubborn hearts', and Simon Peter could never erase from his imagination the gaze of those tender, loving, disappointed eyes as Jesus 'turned and looked straight at Peter' in the high priest's palace just after the cock had crowed (Mark 3:5; Luke 22:60, 61).

In this same letter Jesus calls himself *he who searches hearts and minds* (verse 23). This intimate knowledge of people's secret thoughts and motives is a divine faculty, frequently mentioned in the Old Testament, which *the Son of God* (verse 18) consciously claims to possess. Jeremiah, the prophet to whom was revealed perhaps more clearly than others the inwardness of religion and the importance of the heart, records God's word which Christ here quotes: 'I the LORD search the heart and examine the mind, to reward a man according to his conduct, according to what his deeds deserve.' To this divine claim Jeremiah alludes when he prays: 'O LORD Almighty, you who judge righteously and test the heart and mind ...' So in the Acts of the Apostles God is twice given a name which in the Greek is a single noun, *kardiognōstēs*, 'heart-knower' (Jeremiah 17:10; 11:20; compare 20:12 and Psalm 7:9; Acts 1:24; 15:8).

## Divine insight

The earthly Jesus had this ability too. He read people's thoughts and understood their hearts. Both his enemies and his disciples were amazed at his penetrating insight into the hidden places of their minds. Several times we read, for example, that he 'knew in his spirit that this was what they were thinking in their hearts', so that his closest followers reached the conclusion that nothing could be concealed from him. 'You know all things' was Peter's conviction, while John elaborated it a bit in his words: 'He did not need man's testimony about man, for he knew what was in a man' (Mark 2:8; John 21:17; 2:25). If this clear-sighted scrutiny of the hearts and minds of people was a characteristic of the earthly Jesus, how much more must the risen Christ know all human secrets?

The wicked persuade themselves that their wickedness is not known and will never come to light. 'He does not see', they love to say about God, and 'He will not judge'. But it cannot be stated too emphatically both that God does see and that God will judge. 'Woe to those who go to great depths to hide their plans from the LORD, who do their work in darkness and think, "Who sees us? Who will know?"' 'Nothing in all creation is hidden from God's sight. Everything is uncovered and laid bare before the eyes of him to whom we must give account', and 'God will judge men's secrets through Jesus Christ' (Isaiah 29:15; Hebrews 4:13; Romans 2:16). The people of God need to learn, then, to live in the presence of Christ *whose eyes are like blazing fire* and who *searches hearts and minds* (verses 18, 23). His eyes 'range throughout the earth'. He sees our sitting and our rising, and perceives our thoughts from afar. We cannot escape from his presence. His all-seeing eye is always upon us. To remember this is a most powerful stimulus to holy living. It is what the Bible means by living 'in the fear of the Lord'. (2 Chronicles 16:9; Psalm 139; Proverbs 23:17; 2 Corinthians 7:1.)

## Christ's warning to the Jezebel party

Christ calls on this infamous group in Thyatira to repent. Indeed, they have already had an opportunity to do so, but have not yet availed themselves of it. *I have given her time to repent of her immorality, but she is unwilling* (verse 21). We do not know what warning the Jezebel party may have been given. But we do know that God is 'patient ... not wanting anyone to perish, but everyone to come to repentance'. He has 'no pleasure in the death of anyone'; he 'wants all men to be saved' (2 Peter 3:9; Ezekiel 18:32; 1 Timothy 2:4). This is his wish; but it was not Jezebel's. She 'does not wish to repent', as the Greek phrase of verse 21 should be literally translated.

### Repent!

Jesus Christ does not compel us to surrender, nor forcibly break the stubbornness of our will. He still says to us as he did years ago to impenitent Jerusalem: 'How often I have longed to gather your children together, as a hen gathers her chicks under her wings, but you were not willing' (Matthew 23: 37). If Jezebel would not repent, however, there is still a glimmer of hope for her followers: *those who commit adultery with her* will surely be punished, *unless they repent of their ways* (verse 22). The door of repentance was still open. There was still time. But the opportunity would not last for ever. One day, probably soon, it would pass.

If this final warning was not heeded, judgment would follow. *All the churches will know that I am he who searches hearts and minds, and I will repay each of you according to your deeds* (verse 23). He whose eyes are like blazing fire also has *feet ... like burnished bronze* (verse 18). The eyes that see into the hidden depths of our hearts can also blaze with righteous anger, and his feet can trample us to powder. The nature of the coming judgment of the Jezebel party is couched in highly dramatic and partly symbolical terms. But the imagery must not blind us to the reality. *So I will cast her [Jezebel] on a bed of suffering, and I will make those who commit adultery with her suffer intensely ... I will strike her children dead* (verses 22, 23).

### Judgment

Her punishment will fit her crime. The scene of her wickedness will be the scene of her judgment. Her bed of sin will become a bed of suffering. The pleasures of sin will give place to the pains of affliction, and her spiritual offspring, too deeply dyed with her evil to be cleansed, will be killed. Like the sons of Ahab and Jezebel, they too are doomed. That such literal punishments of illness and death may have overtaken the immoral Jezebel is most likely. This was the epoch in which Ananias and Sapphira fell dead because of their lying hypocrisy, and in which some Corinthian Christians had become ill while others had died because they had defiled the Lord's supper by their greed and irreverence (Acts 5:1–11; 1 Corinthians 11:17–32). In our day similar offenders may not suffer an immediate physical judgment, but Christ's eyes are still like a flame of fire and his feet as strong as burnished brass, and 'the wicked will not inherit the kingdom of God' (1 Corinthians 6:9).

## Christ's advice to the rest

Not all members of the church in Thyatira had been infected with the virus of Jezebel. Some had resisted her contagion. They did *not hold to her teaching.* They had *not learned Satan's so-called deep secrets* (verse 24). In other words, there was a godly remnant in Thyatira who had not defiled themselves. For these, whom Christ describes as *the rest of you in Thyatira* (verse 24), he has a special word of advice. He says first *I will not impose any other burden on you,* and then adds: *only hold on to what you have until I come* (verses 24, 25). This mention of not imposing other burdens appears to be a reference to the apostles' decree promulgated after the Jerusalem Conference described by Luke in Acts 15. The main achievement of this conference was the conclusion that a convert from heathenism did not have to be circumcised. That is, a Gentile did not need to become a Jew in order to be a Christian. On the contrary, in Christ Jews and Gentiles were now equal members of his new community.

Once this great principle had been established, however, there was a willingness to make concessions in certain prac-

**Remains of an early
Christian Basilica at
Akhisar, ancient Thyatira.**

tices. Gentiles were asked to refrain from four things in order
not to offend Jewish consciences. Although there is continuing
debate about these four abstentions, it seems clear that they
were cultural rather than moral. Beyond these cultural concessions, and of course the moral law which was unchanged, the
apostles and elders determined 'not to burden' Gentile believers (Acts 15:28). In the same way, Christ did not wish to 'impose any other burden' on the Thyatiran church; they must
'only hold on to' what they had (verses 24,25), that is, to the
teaching they had already received.

### Glorious liberty
An important lesson lurks in these phrases, which we shall do
well to learn. It is this. A new immorality must not drive us into
a new asceticism. We must not overreact to an extreme laxity
around us by developing an extreme rigidity in ourselves.
Christ has no new burden for those living in an environment
where standards are low. We are simply to hold fast what we
already have, that is to say, what he has already given us in his
written word. What is this? It is the balanced, joyful, exhilarat-
ing righteousness of the Bible, the glorious liberty of the royal
law. It is the same morality which regards the right use of sex
as beautiful and sacred, and its wrong use as ugly and sordid.
It is the teaching which says: 'Marriage should be honoured by
all, and the marriage bed kept pure, for God will judge the
adulterer and all the sexually immoral' (Hebrews 13:4).

69

The Scriptures are a yardstick by which to measure and a criterion by which to test.

God's commandments are not burdensome. Christ's yoke is easy and his burden is light (1 John 5:3; Matthew 11:30). We must not lay upon ourselves or others any other burden beyond his. This is precisely the mistake which the scribes and Pharisees made. They added their own traditions to God's commandments. They tied up 'heavy loads and put them on men's shoulders' (Mark 7:8–13; Matthew 23:4). But the Christian must not play the Pharisee. We are simply to hold fast what we have, that is, what has been given us in the apostles' teaching now recorded in Scripture. Many times the apostles tell us to do just this, to 'see that what you heard from the beginning remains in you', and to 'stand firm and hold to the teachings we passed on to you, whether by word of mouth or by letter' (1 John 2:24; 2 Thessalonians 2:15).

The Holy Scriptures are themselves a 'canon', a yardstick by which to measure and a criterion by which to test. They are an adequate guide and a sufficient rule both of faith and life. Our responsibility is to preserve their teaching and not to add to it.

## Christ's promise to the overcomer

This letter like the others concludes with gracious promises to the overcomer. Indeed, in this case the overcomer is clearly defined as the person who obeys the moral law of Christ. The one *who overcomes* is, in the language of Christ here, the same as the one who *does my will to the end* (verse 26). There are several references in this letter to 'deeds', the deeds by which we cannot be justified but by which we shall certainly be judged (verse 23). Deeds or works are never the ground or means of our salvation, but they are the necessary evidence of it, and therefore they constitute an excellent basis for judgment.

### Two promises
To those who overcome in the fight by keeping Christ's works steadfast to the end, he makes two wonderful promises. Here they are in full. *I will give [him] authority over the nations – He will rule them with an iron sceptre; he will dash them to pieces like pottery – just as I have received authority from my Father. I will also give him the morning star* (verses 26–28). The words I will give occur twice (verses 26 and 28), and echo the same phrase in verse 23. If Christ is going to give to the sinner what his deeds deserve, he will also give to the conqueror far beyond what his deeds could ever begin to deserve. He promises to give the overcomer *authority over the nations* and *the morning star,* which expressions convey the concepts of authority and revelation.

**Reliefs from the theatre at ancient Hierapolis.**

The first promise borrows its imagery from Psalm 2:8,9, where the Messiah's future sovereignty over the nations is remarkably predicted: 'Ask of me,' says God to his Christ, 'and I will make the nations your inheritance, the ends of the earth your possession. You will rule them with an iron sceptre; you will dash them to pieces like pottery' (compare Revelation 12:5; 19:15). This authority Christ now shares with his faithful, overcoming people. *Just as I have received authority from my Father* (verse 27), he says, so I will give authority to you. The quotation from Psalm 2 is slightly modified and adapted. The Greek word for to 'rule' in verse 27 means literally to 'tend'. The potter has become a shepherd, and the nations will not only be pottery to be smashed in pieces, but sheep to be ruled and disciplined in justice.

**Sharing Christ's reign**

Exactly how the overcomer will be permitted to share in Christ's reign is beyond our present state of knowledge. It is enough to remind ourselves that Scripture contains many indications that the new heaven and the new earth will be for the believer a place not only of privilege but of responsibility. The 'good and faithful servant', who has been 'faithful with a few things', will be put 'in charge of many things' and will 'share [his] master's happiness'. Similarly, to the good servant in the Parable of the Ten Minas the nobleman says: 'Because you have been trustworthy in a very small matter, take charge of ten cities'. And Paul adds to the Corinthians: 'Do you not know that the saints will judge the world?' (Matthew 25:21,23; Luke 19:17; 1 Corinthians 6:2). It seems fitting that it should be so. Those who have learned to do Christ's works in this life will continue to do them in the next. Those who have come to rule their own passions on earth will rule over people in heaven.

The second promise of Christ to the overcomer concerns his gift of *the morning star* (verse 28). Many suggestions have been made for the elucidation of this phrase, but as always the word of God is its own best interpreter. In Revelation 22:16 the Lord Jesus describes himself as *the bright Morning Star*. He is also the 'star ... out of Jacob' prophesied by Balaam (Numbers 24:17). The churches may be 'lampstands' and the churches' angels may be described as 'stars', but Christ is the bright morning star from whom they derive their light. In pledging to give this star to the conqueror, then, Christ is pledging to give himself.

Faithful Christians who have repudiated the standards of the world, controlled the desires of their fallen nature and resisted the allurements of the devil will gain this bright morning star. Rejecting Jezebel, they will receive Christ. They will be permitted to share not only in his authority but also in his glory. They will not only rule the nations, but also serve the Lord of the nations. Refusing to dive into the depths of Satan, they will fathom the depths of Christ. Turning their backs on the darkness of sin, they will see the light of the glory of God in the face of Jesus Christ. Christian overcomers, however great their renunciations may have been on earth in the battle for holiness, will with this star, this Christ, remain absolutely and eternally content.

Opposite: The huge
gymnasium at Sardis has
been partially rebuilt in
recent times.

*'You have a reputation of being alive,
but you are dead.'*
Revelation 3:1

The Letter to Sardis:

# Reality

Revelation 3:1–6

The town of Sardis lay about thirty miles south-east of Thyatira and fifty miles due east of Smyrna. Situated at the foot of Mount Tmolus and in the fertile valley of the River Hermus, it was also the converging point of several inland roads, so that it had become a busy centre of trade and traffic. But its ancient history was more distinguished still. The capital of the old kingdom of Lydia, it was here that the fabulous King Croesus reigned amid his treasures until it fell to the swift attack of the Persian conqueror Cyrus.

Inset: An ancient *stela*, or
gravestone.

## Revelation 3:1–6

'To the angel of the church in Sardis write:

These are the words of him who holds the seven spirits of God and the seven stars. I know your deeds; you have a reputation of being alive, but you are dead. ²Wake up! Strengthen what remains and is about to die, for I have not found your deeds complete in the sight of my God. ³Remember, therefore, what you have received and heard; obey it, and repent. But if you do not wake up, I will come like a thief, and you will not know at what time I will come to you.

⁴Yet you have a few people in Sardis who have not soiled their clothes. They will walk with me, dressed in white, for they are worthy. ⁵He who overcomes will, like them, be dressed in white. I will never blot out his name from the book of life, but will acknowledge his name before my Father and his angels. ⁶He who has an ear, let him hear what the Spirit says to the churches.

**The reconstructed gymnasium at Sardis.**

### Sardis in history

Later in its history, Sardis had the distinction of being captured by both Alexander the Great and Antiochus the Great. But it gradually fell on evil days and lost its earlier renown, until in AD 17 it was devastated by an earthquake. Through the generosity of the Emperor Tiberius, who remitted its taxes for five years, the city was rebuilt, and flourished again to the extent that the ancient historian Strabo could call it 'a great city', though it never regained its former glory.

Nothing is known of the origins of the church in Sardis, nor of its early growth, except what may be gathered from this letter.

### A critical letter

The letter which the risen Jesus dictated to John for delivery to the church of Sardis is one of the most severe of the seven. Its criticism is almost unrelieved. 'Like the city itself,' wrote R.H.Charles, 'the church had belied its early promise. Its religious history, like its civil, belonged to the past.' We must consider Christ's message to this church.

# The rebuke Christ gives

Only a few simple words were needed by which to expose this church's spiritual bankruptcy, but they were as devastating as the earthquake of AD 17: *I know your deeds; you have a reputation of being alive, but you are dead* (verse 1). The church of Sardis had acquired a name. Its reputation as a progressive church had evidently spread far and wide. It was well regarded in the city and in the neighbourhood. It was known by the other six churches in the province for its vitality. No false doctrine was taking root in its fellowship. We hear of neither Balaam, nor Nicolaitans, nor Jezebel. 'What a live church you have in Sardis!' visitors would exclaim with admiration when they attended its services or watched its activities; and so no doubt it appeared. Its congregation was probably quite large for those days, and growing, while its programme doubtless included many excellent projects. It had no shortage of money, talent or human resources. There was every indication of life and vigour.

**A spiritual graveyard**

But outward appearances are notoriously deceptive; and this socially distinguished congregation was a spiritual graveyard. It seemed to be alive, but it was actually dead. It had a name for virility, but it had no right to its name. As the eyes of Christ saw beneath the surface, he said: *I have not found your deeds complete in the sight of my God* (verse 2). There were deeds done in the church, but they were not complete, literally 'fulfilled'. They were a routine of duties, but they did not begin to fulfil God's purpose or pattern. The *reputation* that Sardis had acquired was a reputation with human beings – but not with God. It was *in the sight of God*, Christ said, that he had found this church's works deficient. They seemed solid and worthy enough to onlookers, but in God's sight they were thoroughly defective.

This distinction between reputation and reality, between what human beings see and what God sees, is of great importance to every age and place. Although we have responsibilities to others, we are primarily accountable to God. It is before him that we stand, and to him that one day we must give an account. We should not therefore rate human opinion too highly, becoming depressed when criticized and elated when flattered. We need to remember that 'The LORD does not look at the things man looks at. Man looks at the outward appearance, but the LORD looks at the heart' (1 Samuel 16:7). He reads our thoughts and knows our motives. He can see how much reality there is behind our profession, how much life behind our façade.

The ancient synagogue at Sardis has a fine mosaic pavement and coloured stone walls.

## Spiritual death

Another hint is given in the letter to indicate what kind of spiritual death had overtaken Sardis. It is this. The few who did not share in the general stagnation are described as *people ... who have not soiled their clothes* (verse 4). So this death was defilement. Sin had seeped into the church. Although it was less open than in the case of the Jezebel party at Thyatira, Jesus Christ had detected it. Beneath the pious exterior of that respectable congregation was secret uncleanness.

According to the Greek historian Herodotus, the inhabitants of Sardis had over the course of many years acquired a reputation for lax moral standards and even open licentiousness. Perhaps the church in Sardis had forgotten Paul's injunction, 'Do not conform any longer to the pattern of this world' or John's 'Do not love the world or anything in the world' (Romans 12:2; 1 John 2:15). It may be that gradually, even imperceptibly, the yeast of worldliness had spread in the dough, until all of it had become infected.

## Nominal faith

So the reputation of Sardis was false. Indeed, Sardis may have been the first church in the history of Christianity to have been

79

Opposite: The remaining
columns of the Temple of
Artemis (Diana) at Sardis
give an idea of the
grandeur of the original
structure.

characterized by 'nominal Christianity'. Its members belonged to Christ in name, but not in heart. By repute they were alive; in reality they were dead. Jesus himself acknowledged the possibility of being physically alive while spiritually dead when he said that 'the dead' should 'bury their own dead'. Similarly, Paul described unbelievers as 'dead in [their] transgressions and sins', and a frivolous woman as 'dead even while she lives'. Jesus knew that nothing but his own lifegiving voice could awaken such dead people and call them forth from their spiritual graves (Matthew 8:22; Luke 9:60; Ephesians 2:1; 1 Timothy 5:6; John 5:25).

Reality, then, is another essential mark of a true church. A church should have not only *a reputation of being alive* (verse 1) but the life itself. The Bible devotes much space to the differences between outward appearance and inward reality. Amos, Isaiah, Jeremiah and other Old Testament prophets were at pains to teach this distinction to Israel and Judah. The temple and the local sanctuaries teemed with dutiful worshippers. Incense, sacrifices and music were being offered to God with punctilious devotion. But, as Yahweh himself said through Isaiah: 'These people come near to me with their mouth, and honour me with their lips, but their hearts are far from me' (Isaiah 29:13).

### Hypocrites!

Jesus quoted this very saying against the Pharisees, whom he called the successors of those who had rejected and killed the prophets. They gave alms, said long prayers and disfigured their faces to fast, in order to gain a reputation for being religious. In fact, they did all their deeds to be seen by other people, he said. But it was nothing more than a public show. '"Woe to you, teachers of the law and Pharisees, you hypocrites! You are like whitewashed tombs, which look beautiful on the outside but on the inside are full of dead men's bones and everything unclean. In the same way, on the outside you appear to people as righteous but on the inside you are full of hypocrisy and wickedness."' (Matthew 6:1–6, 16–18; 23:5, 27, 28).

Evidently Timothy had come across the same spiritual phenomenon in Ephesus, for Paul wrote to him about some people there as 'having a form of godliness but denying its power' (2 Timothy 3:5). So we can trace this ugly tendency right through the Bible, in both the Old Testament and the New. It is form without power, reputation without reality, outward appearance without inward integrity, show without life.

The correct word for this behaviour is 'hypocrisy'. Originally the *hupokritēs* was an actor, who plays a part on the

stage. But the word came to be applied to any charlatan or pretender who assumes a role. Hypocrisy is make-believe; it is the 'let's pretend' of religion.

And hypocrisy can permeate the life of a church, especially its worship. We can sing the hymns, led by choir and band or orchestra. We can recite the creed, say the confession and join

**The courtyard to the synagogue at Sardis.**

in the prayers, while our mind wanders and our heart is far from God. It makes no difference whether the service is liturgical or non-liturgical, whether it is marked by catholic ritual or protestant austerity; the same unreality can be present.

Pastors are particularly vulnerable. We can lead a service with little awareness of the greatness of the God we are professing to worship. And we can preach rather to display our learning or eloquence than to exalt Christ and minister to the people. But all Christian activity, if it is not an expression of love for God or others, is a hollow mockery and an empty pantomime.

We turn now, with some relief, from the rebuke Christ administered to hypocritical Sardis, to the remedy he proposed to them.

# The remedy Christ proposes

What could be done for a dead church like the one in Sardis? The risen Jesus addresses to it a series of urgent commands. *Wake up! Strengthen what remains and is about to die....* *Remember, therefore, what you have received and heard; obey it and repent* (verses 2–3). Here are five staccato imperatives: Wake up! Strengthen what remains! Remember! Obey! Repent! These orders fall into two parts. The church of Sardis is instructed first to wake up and strengthen what remains, and then to remember its heritage, obey it and repent.

First, *Wake up! Strengthen what remains and is about to die* (verse 2). It is heartening to note that even in dead or moribund Sardis there were some Christians who were not suffering from the general decay. So Christ continues: *Yet you have a few people in Sardis who have not soiled their clothes* (verse 4). In the church's sultry religious torpor a fresh breath of lifegiving air from the Holy Spirit could be felt. Within that worldly congregation a godly remnant was left.

### The godly remnant
It has always been so. In fact, the doctrine of the remnant figures prominently throughout biblical history. Here are some examples. When 'the LORD saw how great man's wickedness on the earth had become, and that every inclination of the thoughts of his heart was only evil all the time', and when he resolved to destroy the inhabitants of the earth by a flood, Noah and his family yet found favour in his sight and were spared. Again, when 'the LORD rained down burning sulphur on Sodom and Gomorrah' and 'overthrew those cities' because of their immorality, 'he rescued Lot, a righteous man, who was distressed by the filthy lives of lawless men'.

Later, when the whole nation of Israel seemed in the days of Ahab and Jezebel to have forsaken Yahweh and turned to Baal, God could reassure Elijah that there were still 'seven thousand in Israel – all whose knees have not bowed down to Baal and all whose mouths have not kissed him'. A century later the southern kingdom of Judah was equally unfaithful to the Lord. Divine judgment brought the nation to the verge of extinction as the countryside was laid waste by invading armies: 'Unless the LORD Almighty had left us some survivors, we would have become like Sodom, we would have been like Gomorrah'. Then the prophet predicted that after the Babylonian exile only a remnant, repentant and purified, would return: 'Though your people, O Israel, be like the sand of the sea, only a remnant will return'. The tree of Israel would be felled, and the 'holy seed' would remain like 'a stump in the land'. So central was this truth to the message of Isaiah that he named one of his sons Shear-Jashub, which means 'a remnant will return'. (Genesis 6:5–18; 19:24, 25; 2 Peter 2:7; 1 Kings 19:18; Isaiah 1:9 (King James Version); 10:20–22; 6:13; 7:3).

Jesus too sometimes spoke of his followers as a kind of remnant. They must not be ashamed of him 'in this adulterous and sinful generation', he said. They were only a 'little flock', but they need not fear, even if when the Son of man comes he will scarcely 'find faith on the earth' (Mark 8:38; Luke 12:32; 18:8).

**A small flock**
To return to Sardis, there were in that city a few Christians who were still loyal in heart and mind to Jesus and who therefore formed a godly remnant. Though the church's name for vigour was deceitful, there were *a few people* (verse 4) who were true. No stigma attached to them. It is to them, therefore, that Christ brings this stirring exhortation to *Wake up! Strengthen what remains and is about to die.* The metaphor has changed from death to sleep. You cannot appeal to a dead man to wake up! But some church members at Sardis were sleepy rather than dead, and the risen Jesus calls them to rouse themselves from their heavy slumbers and to be watchful.

Several times during his public ministry, Jesus told his followers to watch. The word was often on his lips. His disciples must watch and pray; they must be dressed ready for service with their lamps burning, and be like men who are waiting and watching for their master to return from the wedding banquet (Luke 12:35–37).

Some scholars have suggested that the command to be watchful was particularly appropriate to Sardis because this almost impregnable city had twice fallen to surprise attacks, the first time to the Persian Cyrus, and the second to Antiochus the Great. 'Through the failure to watch ... the acropolis had been successfully scaled in 549 BC by a Median soldier, and in 218 by a Cretan' (*International Standard Bible Encyclopaedia*).

### Strengthen what remains

Once awake again, the living remnant of the church were to *strengthen what remains*. The word used for 'strengthen' was often used in the early church for the 'nurture' of believers. For example, Luke describes Paul 'strengthening all the disciples' whom his early preaching and teaching had brought to Christ. Similarly, Paul tells the Christians at Rome that he longs to visit them and 'make [them] strong' in their Christian faith (Acts 18:23; Romans 1:11). Peter and James use the same word in their letters.

New Christians are often weak; they need to be strengthened. They are babes in Christ; they need to be nurtured and loved into maturity. They are usually unstable; they need to become established. Older, maturer Christians have a responsibility to younger ones in the congregation. Stronger Christians must not despise the weak, but encourage and strengthen them by their example, teaching and friendship.

Here then is the duty of the church within the church. God has often worked through minorities. It is his gracious plan to call out from the world and even from the masses of nominal believers a faithful and committed remnant to be his instrument. An alive and awake minority can recall the majority from death. A robust remnant can *strengthen what remains and is about to die* (verse 4).

There is a message here for those who belong to what is sometimes termed 'a dead church', and who are tempted to leave it and go elsewhere. Of course we do have to leave a church which denies the fundamentals of the faith, for then it is apostate and no longer a church. But what about a church which is orthodox but dead? Christ's will in this case is for the living remnant to *strengthen what remains*, perhaps by coming together and waiting upon God. A dynamic minority of awakened and responsible Christians is able by prayer, love and witness both to preserve a dying church from extinction and to fan its flame into a fire.

### Coming judgment

*If you do not wake up* Christ adds, *I will come like a thief, and you will not know at what time I will come to you* (verse 3). Jesus had often issued the warning that his final coming would be as unexpected as a burglar's. This special coming too, in judgment upon an individual church, would be unheralded. As the robbers who lurked in caves in the mountains above Sardis suddenly swooped upon the unwary, so Christ would come. The church's lampstand would be removed; its life would be smothered; its light finally extinguished.

The second set of divine commands to the church in Sardis was: *Remember, therefore, what you have received and heard; obey it, and repent* (verse 3). The ascended Lord had told the church of Ephesus to remember (Revelation 2:5). The church of Sardis is told to remember too. Memory is a precious and blessed gift. Nothing can stab the conscience so wide awake as memories of the past. The shortest road to repentance is remembrance. Let someone once recall what they used to be and reflect on what by God's grace they could be, and they will be led to repent, turning back from their sin to their Saviour.

Moreover, what is true of the individual Christian is true of the local church as a whole. Some churches which today are dead or dying can look back on a long and glorious history. Their older members can call to mind the former days when the congregation was a living fellowship of active workers and people were being regularly added to their number. Let past history challenge us to present endeavour!

But we must be a little more precise. *Remember, therefore, what you have received and heard; obey it ...* (verse 3). What is it which they had received and heard, and which they were to remember? Was it simply the word of God, the gospel? I think not. Sound doctrine on its own cannot reclaim a church from death. Orthodoxy itself can sometimes be dead. They had received more than the gospel. They had received the Holy Spirit. He is the distinctive gift that we all receive when we respond to the gospel with repentance and faith. 'Repent and be baptised, every one of you, in the name of Jesus Christ for the forgiveness of your sins,' cried Peter on the Day of Pentecost, and added: 'and you will receive the gift of the Holy Spirit'. Paul knew this too: 'if anyone does not have the Spirit of Christ, he does not belong to Christ' (Acts 2:38; Romans 8:9).

### The gift of the Spirit

God gives the Spirit; we receive him. Indeed, the greatest gift the Christian has ever received, ever will or could receive, is the Spirit of God himself. He enters our human personality and changes us from within. He fills us with love, joy and peace. He subdues our passions and transforms our characters into the likeness of Christ. Today there is no man-made temple in which God dwells. Instead, his temple is his people. He

inhabits both the individual believer and the Christian community. 'Do you not know,' asks Paul, 'that your body is a temple of the Holy Spirit, who is in you?' Again: 'Do you not know that you yourselves [plural, corporately] are God's temple and that God's Spirit lives in you?' (Galatians 5:22, 23, 16; 2 Corinthians 3:18; 1 Corinthians 6:19; 3:16).

It may well be, then, that Christ is referring to the Holy Spirit when he commands the Christians of Sardis: *Remember, therefore, what you have received* (verse 3). That this is the right interpretation is suggested by the first verse of the letter. Here Jesus describes himself as the one *who holds the seven spirits of God and the seven stars* (verse 1). In every letter his introductory self-description is suited to the condition of the particular church he is addressing. There is no reason to suppose that the letter to Sardis is an exception to this rule. So Sardis is the church which needs to know that the ascended Lord has both *the seven spirits of God and the seven stars.* The seven stars are 'the angels' of the seven churches. Whether these are the churches' presiding ministers or heavenly representatives, they stand for the churches.

### Seven spirits

But who or what are *the seven spirits of God*? The expression is admittedly strange, and yet there can be little doubt that it denotes none other than the Holy Spirit himself. This can be deduced from the first occurrence of the phrase in Revelation 1:4 where grace and peace are desired for the seven churches of Asia 'from him who is, and who was, and who is to come, and from the seven spirits before his throne, and from Jesus Christ ...'. Here the seven spirits are linked with the Eternal Father and with Jesus Christ as the single source of both grace and peace. The closeness of these seven spirits to the throne (Revelation 4:5), and their intimate relation to Jesus Christ (Revelation 5:6), suggest the same conclusion – that they are the Holy Spirit.

Why then is the expression 'seven spirits' used when the Holy Spirit is one person in the Godhead? It will be sufficient to answer with Archbishop Trench 'that he is regarded here not so much in his personal unity as in his manyfold energies'.

So Jesus reminds the church of Sardis that he holds *the seven spirits.* For the Holy Spirit is the Spirit of Christ (Romans 8:9). He was also 'sent' or 'poured out' by Christ on the Day of Pentecost (Acts 2:33).

Now this Spirit of Christ is 'the Spirit of life' (Romans 8:2). As the Nicene Creed declares, he is both 'the Lord' and 'the Lifegiver'. What other message does a dead or moribund church need to hear? It is the Holy Spirit who can breathe life into our formal worship and who can animate our dead works until they pulsate with life. He can rescue a dying church and make it a living force in the community. Let him once fill us with his vital presence, and our work, worship and witness will all be marvellously transformed. The word of God tells us that we must pray in the Spirit, preach in the Spirit, worship in the Spirit, live in the Spirit, and walk in the Spirit (Jude 20; 1 Thessalonians 1:5; John 4:24 and Philippians 3:3; Galatians 5:25, 16). A stale church can be refreshed by him, a sleepy church awakened, a weak church strengthened, and a dead church made alive.

### Seven stars

We notice that the Christ who holds the seven spirits also has the seven stars. Indeed, 'the "spirits" are seven because the churches in which they operate are seven' (Swete). The seven stars, standing in some way for the churches, are in his right hand (Revelation 1:16,20). Are the seven spirits in his left? If only he would bring his hands together! If only the Spirit would fill the church! Christ is willing. Did he not pour out his Spirit upon his church on the Day of Pentecost? The Holy Spirit was given to the church once and for all, and is adequate for all the church's needs. He can never be 'poured out' again,

**Remains of the Temple of Artemis, Sardis.**

for there can be no repetition of the Day of Pentecost. When he came, he came to stay with us for ever (John 14:16). But although he will never withdraw his presence altogether, he can be 'grieved' and even 'quenched' (Ephesians 4:30; 1 Thessalonians 5:19 RSV).

Perhaps there is no more urgent message for twentieth century Christians than the command: 'Be filled with the Spirit' (Ephesians 5:18). He dwells within us; but does he fill us? We possess him; but does he possess us? If we would but submit to the authority of the Spirit, 'keep in step with the Spirit' (Galatians 5:25), and continuously seek the Spirit's fulness, our Christian life would be transformed and our church life revolutionized. In Paul's command to us to be filled, the verb is a present imperative passive. It means 'go on being filled', or even 'be in the state of being filled'. Only when the church of Christ is filled with the Spirit of Christ can spiritual death be banished and a name for life have any reality behind it.

> O Breath of Life, come sweeping through us,
>     Revive your church with life and power;
> O Breath of Life, come, cleanse, renew us
>     And fit your church to meet this hour.

# The reward Christ promises

Once again the letter ends with a promise to the overcomer; and once again the reward promised is appropriate to the church. What Christ offered Sardis had to do with their garments and their name. Many had soiled their clothes; the overcomer would be dressed in white. The church had received a lying name; the overcomer's name would be acknowledged in heaven.

### White clothes
First, *they will walk with me, dressed in white, for they are worthy. He who overcomes will, like them, be dressed in white* (verses 4,5). The majority in Sardis had *soiled their clothes* (verse 4), that is, become defiled by sin, but those who had resisted the evil allurements of the world would wear white clothes and enjoy fellowship with Christ in heaven. White is a frequent colour in this book. We read of a white stone and a white cloud, of white horses and a great white throne (Revelation 2:17; 14:14; 19:11, 14; 20:11). Whether or not white stands for festivity and victory, or has any reference to the use of a white toga by Romans, it certainly symbolizes purity. Of those who are clothed in white, it is written *they are worthy* (verse 4).

Not, however, that the overcomers earn their reward by right, since their forgiveness and moral strength are due to the free grace of Christ alone. No. Their worthiness is borrowed from Christ. The only way to be made fit for entry into God's Kingdom is to be cleansed by Christ who died for us; or, in the rich imagery of this book, to wash our robes and make them white in the blood of the Lamb (Revelation 7:14; compare 22:14).

The distinctive fluted columns of the gymnasium at Sardis are clearly visible in this photograph.

### God's book

Secondly, *I will never blot out his name from the book of life, but will acknowledge his name before my Father and his angels* (verse 5). Scripture tells us that God has a book. Of course it is only a symbol; but behind the symbol is a serious truth. God keeps, as it were, a register in heaven, in which the names of his people are enrolled. It is called 'the book [God] has written', and 'the book of life', since the names of the spiritually dead are not found in it. It is also a 'scroll of remembrance', containing the names of those who 'feared the LORD and honoured his name'. Sometimes it is just 'the book', but more often 'the book of life' or 'the Lamb's book of life' (Exodus 32:32,33; Psalm 69:28; Malachi 3:16; Daniel 12:1; Philippians 4:3 and Revelation 20:15; 13:8 and 21:27).

One day the books will be opened, and the dead will be judged by what is written in the books, and everyone whose name is not found written in the book of life will be 'thrown into the lake of fire' (Revelation 20:11–25).

It is a solemn fact that we can have a reputation for being alive (like the church of Sardis) and still have no entry in God's book of the living. Our name can be on a church register without being on God's register. Jesus told his disciples to rejoice that their names were 'written in heaven' (Luke 10:20; compare Hebrews 12:23).

Christ's gracious promise to the Christian overcomer in Sardis is that he will not blot out his name from the book of life. The Greek sentence has a double negative for emphasis, as if Jesus meant: 'I will never by any means blot out his name'. Indeed, far from removing the overcomer's name from the register of heaven, Christ promises to confess it before his Father and the angels. This is a repetition of what he said during his ministry. 'Whoever acknowledges me before men, I will also acknowledge him before my Father in heaven' and 'before the angels of God' (Matthew 10:32; Luke 12:8).

So this letter closes. We can only hope that the church of Sardis heeded Christ's message to it. Even if they did not, we must. The issues are too serious for us to play the hypocrite. The needs of the world are so great that we cannot afford to dabble in religion or trifle with God. To be given a reputation for life is insufficient; we must possess an inward reality and purity which are known and pleasing to God. We must neither soil our clothes nor betray our name. Filled with the living Spirit of Christ, we can conquer. Then at last we shall wear white garments and walk with Christ in heaven; and our names, indelibly inscribed in the book of life, will be acknowledged before God and the angels.

*Creator Spirit, come, inspire*
*Our lives with light and heavenly fire:*
*Now make us willing to receive*
*The sevenfold gifts you freely give.*

*Your pure anointing from above*
*Is comfort, life and fire of love;*
*So heal with your eternal light*
*The blindness of our human sight.*

*'See, I have placed before you an open door.'*
Revelation 3:8

## The Letter to Philadelphia:

# Opportunity

Revelation 3:7–13

**Minaret of a mosque in Alasehir, ancient Philadelphia.**

**Opposite: 'See, I have placed before you an open door.' Modern Israelis stream through the Damascus Gate to the Old City of Jerusalem.**

The town of Philadelphia was situated about twenty-eight miles south-east of Sardis. It was the next town which the postman would reach on his circular tour of the seven churches of Asia. Like Sardis it was in the fertile region of Lydia and was dominated by Mount Tmolus. It stood on the banks of the River Cogamus, an insignificant tributary of the Hermus. The district was dangerously volcanic. The ancient historian Strabo called Philadelphia 'a city full of earthquakes'. Earth tremors were frequent, and had caused many former inhabitants to leave the city for a safer home. The severe earthquake of AD 17 which devastated Sardis almost completely demolished Philadelphia.

### The church of Philadelphia
But by the 90s, with the aid of an imperial subsidy, Philadelphia had been completely rebuilt, and within the city there was a church of Jesus Christ. To it the sixth of the seven letters is

---

### Revelation 3:7–13

'To the angel of the church in Philadelphia write:

These are the words of him who is holy and true, who holds the key of David. What he opens no-one can shut, and what he shuts no-one can open. [8]I know your deeds. See, I have placed before you an open door that no-one can shut. I know that you have little strength, yet you have kept my word and have not denied my name. [9]I will make those who are of the synagogue of Satan, who claim to be Jews though they are not, but are liars – I will make them come and fall down at your feet and acknowledge that I have loved you. [10]Since you have kept my

command to endure patiently, I will also keep you from the hour of trial that is going to come upon the whole world to test those who live on the earth.

[11]I am coming soon. Hold on to what you have, so that no-one will take your crown. [12]Him who overcomes I will make a pillar in the temple of my God. Never again will he leave it. I will write on him the name of my God and the name of the city of my God, the new Jerusalem, which is coming down out of heaven from my God; and I will also write on him my new name. [13]He who has an ear, let him hear what the Spirit says to the churches.

addressed, in which the ascended Christ expresses warm approval of his people. The previous letter to Sardis contained almost unmitigated censure. The letter to Philadelphia is one of almost unqualified commendation. *I know your works* (verse 8), he begins, as in each letter, and continues a little later: *you have kept my word and have not denied my name* (verse 8). Again, *you have kept my command to endure patiently* (verse 10).

Evidently, there had been some recent persecution in Philadelphia, but the Christians (though hard pressed) had held fast their profession. As in Pergamum, where Antipas had been cruelly martyred, so in Philadelphia, the Christians had courageously stood their ground (compare Revelation 2:13). They were patiently bearing tribulation and shame for Christ's sake. In Jesus Christ they were sharing with the exiled John *the suffering and kingdom and patient endurance* (Revelation 1:9).

This letter to the Philadelphian church is particularly striking on account of its vivid symbolical descriptions. In it we read of a key, a door and a pillar. The church is described as having had set before it *an open door that no-one can shut* (verse 8); Christ is called the One *who holds the key of David* (verse 7); while the overcomer will be made a *pillar in the temple of my God* (verse 12). We must consider carefully the exciting relationship which exists between the church's open door, Christ's master key and the heavenly pillar.

# The church and the open door

*See,* says Jesus, *I have placed before you an open door that no-one can shut* (verse 8). What is this door which has been opened wide and cannot be closed? Often in Scripture an open door is a door of opportunity. Then, when the door is closed, the opportunity has passed. The metaphor is used in two main senses.

### The opportunity of salvation
The first open door is the opportunity of salvation. Some commentators think that this is the meaning in the Philadelphian letter. The context makes this suggestion unlikely. Nevertheless the picture is so clear in other parts of the Bible that we can hardly omit it from consideration. Jesus himself twice used this language. During the Sermon on the Mount he said: 'Enter through the narrow gate. For wide is the gate and broad is the road that leads to destruction, and many enter through it. But small is the gate and narrow the way that leads to life, and only a few find it' (Matthew 7:13,14).

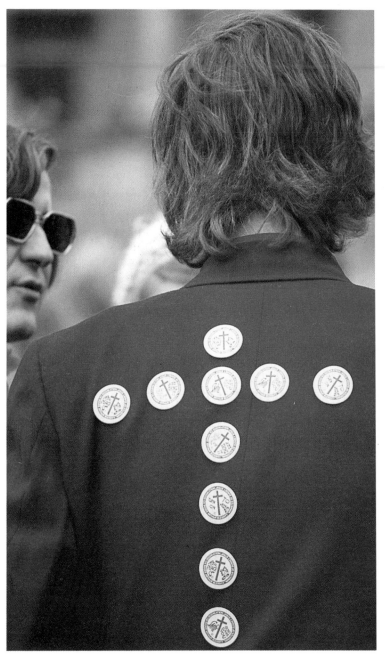

**Jesus teaches that the gate leading to life is small, and the way narrow.**

Here are two gates, and both are open. One opens onto a broad and crowded thoroughfare, which slopes gently downwards and ends in the destruction called hell. The other door opens onto a sparsely populated and narrow path, which winds steeply upwards and leads to eternal life.

Jesus' teaching is plain but unfashionable. He contrasts not only two ways and two ends, but two gates. Both are open and inviting, although one is wide and the other narrow. The wide gate is so spacious that it is easy for carefree people to surge through it in large numbers. But the other gate is so low that we have to stoop humbly to enter it, and so narrow that we can only just squeeze through one at a time. There is no room to take anything with us. Our sins and selfishness have to be left behind.

Thus, although one door is wide and the other low and narrow, and although many are thronging through the one, while only a few slip quietly through the other, both doors stand open inviting people to enter.

### The opportunity of service

The second kind of open door is the opportunity of service. It is important to add this. Otherwise we give the impression that we are interested only in our own salvation. Mark Guy Pearce spoke a wise and true word when he said: 'Unless our faith saves us out of selfishness into service, it will certainly never save us out of hell into heaven'. Christian believers who have received salvation as a free gift from God through Jesus Christ are deeply concerned about the material and spiritual welfare of their fellow human beings. Having gone in through the door of salvation, they hurry out through the door of service to look for others and (in the words of Jesus) 'compel them to come in'.

### A great door for effective work

It seems certain that the door which stood open before the Philadelphian church was the door of opportunity. Openings for the spread of the gospel were many and great in the Roman Empire of the first century AD. The *Pax Romana* permitted Christian evangelists to go about their business with comparative freedom, speaking the common Greek language, treading the fine Roman roads and using as their textbook the Septuagint (Greek) version of the Old Testament. In addition, wherever they went, they found groping minds and hungry hearts. The old pagan superstitions were being abandoned. The Holy Spirit was stirring the thoughts and desires of ordinary men and women. Many thirsty souls were panting for the water of life. Paul found this everywhere.

On the third of his famous missionary journeys the apostle spent three years in Ephesus, giving public lectures in a hired hall and visiting people privately in their own homes. Night and day he was busy preaching the gospel. Of this period he wrote: 'a great door for effective work has opened to me' (1 Corinthians 16:9). When later he reached Rome, the capital of the known world, and was for two years kept under house arrest, he yet spoke of Christ to all who visited him – Jews, Roman soldiers, and a runaway slave called Onesimus. Yet all

**Remains of the early Christian basilica at Alasehir, ancient Philadelphia.**

these opportunities were not enough for him. 'Pray for us, too,' he wrote to his Christian friends in Colossae, 'that God may open a door for our message, so that we may proclaim the mystery of Christ, for which I am in chains. Pray that I may proclaim it clearly, as I should.' (Colossians 4:3,4; compare 2 Corinthians 2:12).

### Fierce opposition

In Philadelphia too a door had been opened by Christ. Yet, as in Ephesus so in Philadelphia, in addition to the open door there were many problems (see 1 Corinthians 16:9). Three are implied. For one thing, the Philadelphian church was pathetically weak. *I know that you have little strength* (verse 8), says Christ. Perhaps the congregation was small, or perhaps it was composed largely of the lower classes of Roman society, so that it had little influence on the city. This was not to deter them from evangelism, however. Secondly, there was opposition, which, as in Smyrna (Revelation 2:9), appears to have come from the Jewish population of the city. So fanatical was their resistance to the gospel of their Messiah, that they are again called a synagogue not of God but of Satan, *who claim to be Jews though they are not, but are liars* (verse 9).

The fierceness of this opposition probably tempted the

Philadelphian Christians to hold their peace and mind their own business. Perhaps some church members counselled that discretion was the better part of valour and that Christians should not stir up trouble. But Christ was of another mind. It was in this very city where Jewish antagonism was so strong that he opened a door for the gospel. Indeed, he makes it clear that if only his people would move out boldly with the good news, some of those who would receive it would be Jews! *I will make those* [literally, some] *who are of the synagogue of Satan ... come and fall down at your feet and acknowledge that I have loved you* (verse 9).

Jewish converts are here portrayed as captives on the battlefield. They themselves would be familiar with this imagery. It had been prophesied of them years before that 'the sons of your oppressors will come bowing before you; all who despise you will bow down at your feet' (Isaiah 60:14). But now the tables are turned. Instead of Gentiles kneeling at Jewish feet, Jews will bow down before Christians – not of course to worship them, but humbly to recognize the community of Jesus as the new and the true Israel on whom God has set his love.

**The threat of persecution**
The third obstacle in the path of the Philadelphian Christians was the threat of future tribulation. The thunder clouds of persecution were gathering. At any time the storm might break. Surely this was no time for evangelism? Was it not a time for retrenchment and consolidation, rather than for advance? Again, Christ has different ideas. With one breath he warns them of coming trial, and with the next urges them to step through the open door without fear. Moreover, he promises *I will also keep you from the hour of trial that is going to come upon the whole world to test those who live on the earth* (verse 10). Had they kept his word? Then he would keep them from harm. He would not spare them from the suffering; but he would uphold them in it.

In contrast to the Philadelphian believers, how easily do we modern Christians give up! Subtle and specious are the excuses we give for avoiding the challenge of evangelism. Our forces are small and feeble, we say. The opposition is great, and the danger of further unpleasantness real. So let us not do anything rash or foolish. Let us wait a while until the circumstances become more favourable. Does not the Bible itself say: 'There is a time to speak and a time to be silent'? Yes, indeed, but the devil himself is adept at misquoting and misapplying Scripture. Neither the church's weakness nor present nor future opposition should silence us. The Philadelphian church had all these

**Relief from the ancient theatre of Perga, Asia Minor.**

handicaps; yet it was before this church that Jesus Christ opened the door of service.

He could already say to them: *you have kept my word and have not denied my name* (verse 8). But these negative stances were no substitute for positive evangelistic witness! Had the Philadelphians kept Christ's word? Let them now begin to spread it! Had they refused to deny Christ's name? Let them now actively proclaim it!

### A strategic location

We cannot say for certain in what sense Christ had opened a door for the gospel in Philadelphia. But perhaps, as some scholars have suggested, the church's unusual opportunities were due to the city's geographical location. According to Sir William Ramsay, the intention of the city's founder in the second century BC had been 'to make it a centre of the Graeco-Asiatic civilization and a means of spreading the Greek language and manners in the eastern parts of Lydia and in Phrygia. It was a missionary city from the beginning ...' What the city had been for Greek culture, it was now to be for the Christian gospel. It was built on one of the great Roman roads which thrust its way like an arrow into the heart of the interior. Philadelphia was on the borders of Mysia, Lydia and Phrygia, and Ramsay describes it as being 'the keeper of the gateway' to the central plateau and 'on the threshold of the eastern country'. The Philadelphian church seems to have had the chance to spread far and wide the good news of God's grace and kingdom. The door was open. No-one could shut it. Let them pass through!

**Open doors**

The same is true of the Christian church in many parts of the world today. True, some doors are closed; but very many are open. There are more vacancies than can be filled, and more opportunities than can be taken. There is a shortage of people of the right kind. There is a lack of men and women who are on the one hand trained and competent, and on the other wholly committed to Christ. The church urgently needs Christians of apostolic zeal who will count all things loss for Christ, and hazard life, comfort, career and reputation for him. The open doors are many; but there are few to go through them.

Here then is the balance of the Christian life. It is a life of give and take. 'Freely you have received,' said Jesus, 'freely give.' First we gratefully take what he offers; then we gladly give what he asks. He sets before us the open doors of salvation and of service. He bids us go in through the one to receive salvation and out through the other to give service. It is not possible to go through the second until we have been through the first. As Jesus put it: 'I am the gate; whoever enters through me will be saved. He will come in and go out, and find pasture.' (John 10:9).

# Christ and the key of David

Before telling the Philadelphian church about the open door which he has set before them, Jesus begins his letter with these significant statements: *These are the words of him who is holy and true, who holds the key of David. What he opens no-one can shut, and what he shuts no-one can open* (verse 7). To begin with, he is self-consciously divine. 'The Holy One' is a title which Yahweh gave himself in the Old Testament (see for instance Isaiah 40:25). Jesus now assumes it naturally and without any fuss. He is not only holy; he is true. He hates all evil and error. He is the perfection of righteousness and the fulfilment of all prophecy. And one of the shadowy predictions of the Old Testament which he has fulfilled is mentioned here. It concerns *the key of David* which he claims to possess. We turn in thought from the open door to the key which opened it. The reason why the door stands open before the church is that its key is in the hand of Christ.

### The key of David

The language is borrowed from Isaiah 22 where it is used of a man named Eliakim. He was one of the three delegates chosen to negotiate for the kingdom of Judah with the Assyrian Rabshakeh. This was doubtless because of the honourable position he occupied in the palace. He had been made steward over King Hezekiah's household. God gave him this authority, calling him 'a father to those who live in Jerusalem', and added: 'I will place on his shoulder the key to the house of David; what he opens no-one can shut, and what he shuts no-one can open' (2 Kings 18:17,18; Isaiah 22:21,22).

It is not very difficult to see that Eliakim prefigured or foreshadowed Jesus Christ; for Christ is the head of God's household, the church. He is the 'true' steward, of whom Eliakim was the prototype, and he is 'faithful ... over God's house'. To him God has given 'all authority in heaven and on earth' (Hebrews 3:6; Matthew 28:18). It is he therefore who has the keys, not only 'of death and Hades' (Revelation 1:18), but also of salvation and of service. No-one can enter until Christ has opened the door. Nor can anyone enter when he closes it. He says of himself, as God said of Eliakim, that *what he opens no-one can shut, and what he shuts no-one can open* (verse 7). So, if the door is the symbol of the church's opportunity, the key is the symbol of Christ's authority.

**The Damascus Gate into the Old City of Jerusalem is today one of the busiest entrances.**

103

## The key of salvation

First, Christ holds the key to the door of salvation. Do we wish to enter the narrow door and step onto the narrow way which leads to life? Jesus Christ has the key. None but he can open this door. We note in passing that the key is in the hand of Christ, and not in the hand of Peter. Jesus certainly said to Peter: 'I will give you the keys of the kingdom of heaven' (Matthew 16:19). And Peter used them. It was through his proclamation of the gospel that the first Jews were converted on the day of Pentecost; through the laying on of his hands (with John) that the Holy Spirit was given to the first Samaritan believers; and through his ministry that the first Gentiles, Cornelius the Roman centurion and his household, heard the gospel, believed and were baptized. By the use of the keys committed to him, Peter thus opened the kingdom of heaven to the first Jews, the first Samaritans and the first Gentiles (Acts 2:14–41; 8:14–17; 10:44–48). But now the keys are back in the hands of Christ, and if human beings use them at all today it is only in the secondary sense that they are privileged to preach the gospel through which sinners believe and are saved.

The key of salvation is in the hand of Christ. Indeed, he has 'opened the gate of heaven to all believers'. *I have placed before you an open door* (verse 8), he says. The tense is perfect, for he opened it once for all long ago, and it still stands open today. How is this so? It is because at the threshold of the narrow door there stands a cross. On it our Saviour died for us. He had no sins of his own; he bore our sins in his own body. He did not deserve to die; he took our deserts. He accepted in his own innocent person the judgment which our sins had righteously deserved. That is why the gate is open. Any sinner may now enter the inner sanctuary of God's presence, and do so with confidence, 'by the blood of Jesus, by a new and living way opened for us through the curtain, that is, his body' (Hebrews 10:19,20).

We may have wandered for many weary years in the bypaths of aimlessness. But now we may set our foot on the highway which leads to glory! Christ is the living one, who died and rose and has the keys of death. He says *I have placed before you an open door that no-one can shut* (verse 8). But one day it will be shut. Christ himself will shut it. For the key which unlocked it will lock it again. And when he shuts it, no-one can open it. Both admission and exclusion are in his power alone.

## A locked door

Many people find it hard to accept that anybody will ever be excluded. They need to listen to Christ's own words: 'Make every effort to enter through the narrow door, because many, I tell you, will try to enter and will not be able to. Once the

owner of the house gets up and closes the door, you will stand outside knocking and pleading, "Sir, open the door for us."

'But he will answer, "I don't know you or where you come from."

'Then you will say, "We ate and drank with you, and you taught in our streets."

'But he will reply, "I don't know you or where you come from. Away from me, all you evildoers!"

'There will be weeping there, and gnashing of teeth, when you see Abraham, Isaac and Jacob and all the prophets in the kingdom of God, but you yourselves thrown out' (Luke 13:24–28).

Those of us who are churchgoers need, in particular, to heed these solemn words of Jesus. For on the last day we could find ourselves battering at a door which is kept closed against us, while Jesus says 'I don't know you'. We may respond indignantly, 'But we ate and drank in your presence; we took the bread and sipped the wine at holy communion. You taught us too. We sat in the pews and listened to your word.' But again he may say, 'I don't know you or where you come from.' In other words, it is possible to be a baptized, communicant Christian and still remain outside the door of salvation. We have to come to Jesus and say:

Just as I am, without one plea
but that you died to set me free,
and at your bidding 'Come to me!'
 O Lamb of God, I come.

Once we have knelt humbly before the cross, we are ready to rise to our feet and step quickly through the door before it is too late.

### The key of service
Secondly, Christ holds the key to the door of service. There is little question that the men and women of the Bible had a keener sense than we have of the sovereignty of God in the world. They did not believe that human beings had the right to force closed doors and break in. This is plain in both the Old and the New Testaments. Was it a question of the military career of the Persian conqueror Cyrus? 'This is what the LORD says to his anointed, to Cyrus, whose right hand I take hold of to subdue nations before him and to strip kings of their armour, to open doors before him so that gates will not be shut: I will go before you and will level the mountains; I will break down gates of bronze and cut through bars of iron.' Or, was the apostle Peter miraculously released from Herod's

prison in answer to the church's prayers so that his chains fell off his hands? Then, led by an angel past the first and second guard, 'the iron gate leading to the city ... opened for them by itself'. Again, did Paul and Barnabas on the first missionary journey travel over land and sea, hill and valley, mountain and swamp? Were they abused, hated and stoned and yet given grace to win many for Christ? Then they had an explanation. On their return to Antioch, 'they gathered the church together and reported all that God had done through them and how he had opened the door of faith to the Gentiles' (Isaiah 45:1,2; Acts 12:1–11; 14:27).

Christ has the keys. He opens the doors. There is no sense in trying to barge our way unceremoniously through doors which are still closed. We have to wait for him to make openings for us. Damage is continually being done to the cause of Christ by brash or tactless testimony. It is of course right to seek to win for Christ our friends, relatives, neighbours and colleagues. But we are sometimes in a greater hurry than God. Instead, we need to be patient, pray hard and love much, and to wait expectantly for the God-given opportunity to witness.

The same principle applies to any uncertainty we may have about God's will for our future. Probably more mistakes are made by speed than by sloth, by impatience than by delay. God's purposes often ripen slowly. If the door is shut, it is foolish to put our shoulder to it. We must wait till Christ takes out the key and opens it.

### 'Come over ... and help us'

But of course many doors are already standing wide open. Christ has used his keys. He has turned many locks and drawn many bolts. He has opened many doors, and on the other side are the millions who still beckon us and say, 'Come over ... and help us.'

We must not turn a deaf ear to their appeal. All Christians should be global Christians in the sense that we are strongly committed to world evangelization. Of course, not all of us are called to go through the open doors ourselves as cross-cultural messengers of the gospel. But we all have a responsible share, especially by our prayers, gifts and encouragement, to ensure that the open doors are entered.

We must also be local as well as global Christians, concerned for the district in which our church is situated, and in this mission all of us should have a part. This was Christ's message to Philadelphia. His words were addressed neither to an individual, nor to ordained or other leaders, nor to a select circle within the fellowship, but to the whole church. It was before the whole church of Philadelphia that he had opened a door. Evangelism is not the prerogative of pastors or other professionals. It is not the hobby of a few fanatics. It is a duty resting upon the whole congregation and upon every member of it.

Not only is every individual Christian called to be a witness, but every local Christian community is called to mobilize its membership for mission. This will involve a careful training programme, the regular visitation of the whole neighbourhood, the development of home evangelism and the arrangement of special events at which the gospel is shared. These are some of the doors which Christ has opened. We must make sure we go through them. The key is Christ's; but the choice is ours.

# The overcomer as a pillar in God's temple

Once more Christ is not content merely to exhort. To his admonitions he adds promises. *I am coming soon,* he says; *Hold on to what you have, so that no-one will take your crown* (verse 11). Let the Christians in Philadelphia stand firm as well as move forward. Let no enemy rob them of their reward. Then comes the special pledge to the overcomer. *Him who overcomes I will make a pillar in the temple of my God. Never again will he leave it. I will write on him the name of my God and the name of the city of my God, the new Jerusalem, which is coming down out of heaven from my God; and I will also write on him my new name* (verse 12). What could be more appropriate to the active evangelists in Philadelphia? The same promise applies to us. If we renounce in this life the way of ease, we shall in the next life, in God's temple which is heaven, be made pillars, stable, immovable, secure, which would not fall even if Samson were to lean on them. Philadelphian Christians might live in fear of earthquake shocks, but nothing will shake them when they stand as pillars in heaven.

### To be a pilgrim

If, then, we become a pilgrim in this life, we will be a pillar in the next. If we dare to go out through the door of service, we will never go out of the security of paradise. If we risk our name for Christ in this world, then on our pillar in the next, three names will be permanently engraved. The first will be the name of God, the second the name of the New Jerusalem (the church triumphant), and the third Christ's own new name. That is to say (since the name stands for the one named), we shall belong for ever to God, to Christ and to his people, and shall continually grow in our knowledge of them. That is the

prospect before all those who go forth valiantly through open doors, wage war against the powers of evil, and conquer in the fight. It is the promise of Christ; it is true.

As we conclude our study of this sixth letter, we acknowledge its relevance to our own day. The open door stands for the church's opportunity; the key of David for Christ's authority; and the pillar of God's temple for the overcomer's security. Christ has the keys. Christ has opened the doors. Christ promises to make us safe as massive pillars in God's temple. Now it is up to us. The doors stand open still. Christ invites us first to go in through the door of salvation, and then to go out through the door of service.

*'You are lukewarm –
neither hot nor cold'*
Revelation 3:16

## The Letter to Laodicea:

# Wholeheartedness

Revelation 3:14–22

In each of the seven letters Jesus Christ lays emphasis on a different mark which should characterize a true and living church. The Ephesian Christians are urged to return to their first, fresh love for him, while the Christians of Smyrna are warned that if they do not compromise they will surely suffer. The church in Pergamum is to champion truth in the face of error, and the church in Thyatira righteousness in the midst of evil. In Sardis the need is for inward reality behind the church's outward show. Before the Philadelphian church the risen Lord has set an open door of opportunity for the spread of the gospel, and he bids them step boldly through it. The seventh letter is addressed to the church in Laodicea; it combines a fierce denunciation of complacency with a tender appeal for wholeheartedness.

### Revelation 3:14–22

'To the angel of the church in Laodicea write:

These are the words of the Amen, the faithful and true witness, the ruler of God's creation. [15] I know your deeds, that you are neither cold nor hot. I wish you were either one or the other! [16] So, because you are lukewarm – neither hot nor cold – I am about to spit you out of my mouth. [17] You say, 'I am rich; I have acquired wealth and do not need a thing.' But you do not realise that you are wretched, pitiful, poor, blind and naked. [18] I counsel you to buy from me gold refined in the fire, so that you can become rich; and white clothes to wear, so that you can cover your shameful nakedness; and salve to put on your eyes, so that you can see.

[19] Those whom I love I rebuke and discipline. So be earnest, and repent. [20] Here I am! I stand at the door and knock. If anyone hears my voice and opens the door, I will come in and eat with him, and he with me.

[21] To him who overcomes, I will give the right to sit with me on my throne, just as I overcame and sat down with my Father on his throne. [22] He who has an ear, let him hear what the Spirit says to the churches.'

Part of the famous limestone cliffs deposited by the lukewarm water at Hierapolis, opposite the site of ancient Laodicea.

## Laodicea

About forty miles south-east of Philadelphia three famous cities clustered in the valley of the River Lycus. North of the river stood Hierapolis, while on its south bank were situated Laodicea and Colossae, about ten miles distant from each other. Laodicea was thus the most southerly of the seven churches to which these letters were addressed, being almost due east of Ephesus.

Although Laodicea was the chief city of the southern region of Phrygia and had no small distinction, nobody knows when

the seeds of the gospel were sown in it or how the church took root there. The apostle Paul probably never visited the cities of the Lycus valley, but he wrote a letter to the Laodicean church at the same time as he wrote his letter to the Colossians. Indeed, many scholars think that the Laodicean letter is none other than our so-called 'Letter to the Ephesians', since three of the best and earliest manuscripts of that letter omit at its beginning the words, 'at Ephesus'. It may therefore have been a circular letter, which was sent in the first instance to Laodicea. Further, the double mention of Epaphras in the Letter to the Colossians indicates both that he had evangelized Colossae and that he had links with Laodicea as well. So perhaps it was he who founded the Laodicean church (Colossians 1:7; 2:1; 4:12–16).

### A stern letter

Whenever it was founded, and however it may have prospered in its early history, the church in Laodicea has by John's day fallen on evil days. Consequently, Jesus sends it the sternest of the seven letters, containing much censure and no praise. It had not been infected with the poison of any special sin or error. We read neither of heretics, nor of evil-doers, nor of persecutors. But the Christians in Laodicea are *neither cold nor hot* (verse 15). They lack wholeheartedness, so that the adjective 'Laodicean' has passed into our vocabulary to describe somebody who is lukewarm in religion or politics or any other sphere.

Perhaps none of the seven letters is more appropriate to the church at the end of the twentieth century than this. It describes vividly the respectable, nominal, rather sentimental, skin-deep religiosity which is so widespread among us today. Our Christianity is flabby and anaemic. We appear to have taken a lukewarm bath of religion. In this phrase there is probably 'an allusion to the hot springs of Hierapolis, which in their way over the plateau become lukewarm, and in this condition discharge themselves over the cliff right opposite Laodicea' (Swete).

### On fire for Christ

Laodicean religion is like a lukewarm waterfall. But Jesus Christ deserves better treatment than this. He wants his followers to be either cold or hot. *I know your deeds,* he says; *you are neither cold nor hot. I wish you were either one or the other!* (verse 15). The Greek words are striking, and we are left in no doubt about their meaning. 'Cold' means icy cold and 'hot' means boiling hot. Jesus Christ would prefer us to boil or freeze, rather than that we should simmer down into a tasteless

A few stone arches are all that remain today of the stadium of ancient Laodicea.

tepidity. Paul told the Roman Christians to be what he had found Apollos to be, namely 'fervent in spirit' (King James Version) – or spiritually at boiling point. We are to 'maintain the spiritual glow', as Moffatt translated this exhortation, and to 'stir into flame' the gift of God that is in us. Our inner spiritual fire is in constant danger of dying down. It needs to be poked and fed and fanned into flame (Romans 12:11; Acts 18:25; 2 Timothy 1:6).

The idea of being on fire for Christ will strike some people as dangerous emotionalism. 'Surely,' they will say, 'we are not meant to go to extremes? You are not asking us to become hot-gospel fanatics?' Well, of course, it depends what you mean. If by 'fanaticism' you really mean 'wholeheartedness', then Christianity is a fanatical religion and every Christian should be a fanatic. But wholeheartedness is not the same as fanaticism. Fanaticism is an unreasoning and unintelligent wholeheartedness. It is the running away of the heart with the head. At the end of a statement prepared for a conference on science, philosophy and religion at Princeton University in 1940 came these words: 'Commitment without reflection is fanaticism in action; but reflection without commitment is the paralysis of all action.' What Jesus Christ desires and deserves is the reflection which leads to commitment and the commitment which is born of reflection. This is the meaning of wholeheartedness, of being aflame for God.

### A time for enthusiasm

One longs to see today robust and courageous men and women bringing to Jesus Christ their thoughtful and total commitment. He asks for this. He even says that if we will not be hot, he would prefer us cold to lukewarm. Better to be frigid than tepid, he implies. His meaning is not far to seek. If he is true; if he is the Son of God who became a human being, died for our sins, and was raised from death; if Christmas Day, Good Friday and Easter Day are more than meaningless anniversaries, then nothing less than our wholehearted commitment to Christ will do. This means that we will put him first in our private and public life, seeking his glory and obeying his will. Better be icy in our indifference or go into active opposition to him than insult him with an insipid compromise which nauseates him!

True, the Christian church has often been scared of 'enthusiasm'. John Wesley and his friends had reason to know that. So have many others both before him and since. But enthusiasm is an essential part of Christianity. Christ warmly approves of it even if the church disapproves. His message to us in our sleepy-headed lethargy and chilliness is the same as his message to Laodicea years ago: *be earnest, and repent* (verse 19). Earnestness, zeal, fervour, fire, passion – these are the qualities we lack today and greatly need.

We must consider carefully what Christ says about half-heartedness as he explains what it is, how to overcome it and the reward he promises to the wholehearted.

## The diagnosis Christ makes

We shall need to brace ourselves to hear what Jesus thinks of the Laodicean church. Here are his words: *You say, 'I am rich; I have acquired wealth and do not need a thing.' But you do not realise that you are wretched, pitiful, poor, blind and naked* (verse 17). This is the diagnosis of the Good Physician. The tepid person is someone in whom there is a glaring contrast between what he says and thinks he is on the one hand and what he really is on the other. The root cause of half-heartedness is complacency. To be lukewarm is to be blind to one's true condition.

### An opulent society

No doubt the congregation of Laodicea teemed with self-satisfied churchgoers. They said *I am rich; I have acquired wealth and do not need a thing.* They were quite right – in material terms. Laodicea was renowned for its prosperity. Situated in a

fertile valley at the junction of several important trade routes, it had amassed considerable wealth. So opulent were its citizens that, when the earthquake of AD 60 devastated the whole region, the city was promptly rebuilt without any appeal to the Roman senate for the customary subsidy. The local inhabitants were proud of their city as a mercantile banking centre. They could boast of its famous medical school connected with the temple of Aesculapius 'whose physicians prepared the Phrygian powder for the cure of ophthalmia', which was described by Aristotle. Particularly well-known was their manufacture of cloth, garments and carpets from the valuable wool of the local sheep, which William Ramsay says was 'soft in texture and glossy black in colour'.

The pride of Laodicea was infectious. Christians caught the plague. The spirit of complacency crept into the church and tainted it. Church members became smug and self-satisfied, and Jesus Christ needed to be blunt in exposing them. He did not mince his words. *You say, 'I am rich; I have acquired wealth and do not need a thing.' But you do not realise that you are wretched, pitiful, poor, blind and naked* (verse 17). They thought they were doing fine in their religious life. But Christ had to describe them as blind and naked beggars – beggars despite their banks, blind despite the Phrygian powders of their medical school, and naked despite their clothing factories. *I ... do not need a thing,* they said. They could indeed manage without an imperial subsidy; but they could not manage without the grace of Jesus Christ.

### Naked, blind beggars

This then is Christ's view of us – of nominal Christians who are neither really nor wholeheartedly committed to him. Morally and spiritually such people are naked, blind beggars. They are beggars because they have nothing with which to purchase their forgiveness or an entry into the Kingdom of God. They are naked because they have no clothes to fit them to stand before God. They are blind because they have no idea either of their spiritual poverty or of their spiritual danger.

Such is the ascended Christ's penetrating diagnosis of our spiritual condition. We would be foolish to resist it. To contradict the considered judgment of a skilled physician is the surest road to disaster. *I know your deeds* he says, and adds *you do not realise ...* (verses 15 and 17). He knows us better than we know ourselves. We tend to flatter and deceive ourselves, but he sees and knows us as we really are.

# The advice Christ gives

*I counsel you ...* (verse 18). Perhaps we could first observe the fact that we have a God who is content to give advice to his creatures. I can never read this verse without being strangely moved. He is the great God of the expanding universe. He has countless galaxies of stars at his fingertips. The heaven and the heaven of heavens cannot contain him. He is the creator and sustainer of all things, the Lord God Almighty. He has the right to issue orders for us to obey. He prefers to give advice which we need not heed. He could command; he chooses to counsel. He respects the freedom with which he has ennobled us.

At the same time he warns us of the serious consequences of our complacency. His purpose is not to terrify us into submission, but to make us aware of the solemnity of our choice. *Because you are lukewarm – neither hot nor cold – I am about to spit you out of my mouth* (verse 16). It is of course metaphorical language, but this does not empty the expression of its meaning. Lukewarm liquids create nausea. They are not only tasteless but positively distasteful. Christ's forceful expression is one of disgust. He will utterly repudiate those whose attachment to him is purely nominal and superficial. One is reminded of the description in Psalm 95 of God's attitude to Israel in the wilderness: 'For forty years I was angry with that generation' (verse 10). The verb used is almost shocking. The Revised Standard Version translates it 'loathed'. Not that God's wrath is ever tinged with personal malice, spite or vindictiveness. But the Hebrew word here conveys distaste and disgust, and indicates God's strong moral revulsion to human hypocrisy and sin.

## Desolation and waste

Whether or not the Laodicean church heeded this warning we cannot say. Certainly the city, once prosperous and complacent, is now a miserable waste. 'Nothing can exceed the desolation and melancholy appearance of the site of Laodicea' says a twentieth-century traveller. Archbishop Trench vividly portrays the scene: 'All has perished now. He who removed the candlestick of Ephesus, has rejected Laodicea out of his mouth. The fragments of aqueducts and theatres spread over a vast extent of country tell of the former magnificence of this city; but of this once famous church nothing survives.'

It is not only, however, through fear of judgment that we should heed this divine warning, but also from respect for the One who issues it. See how he describes himself in the introduction to this letter: *The words of the Amen, the faithful and true witness, the ruler of God's creation* (verse 14). He is the

Amen. This Hebrew word is an adverb of assent. It means 'indeed' or 'truly', and denotes the confirmation of something said or done. It is the word employed by Jesus in his favourite formula: 'Truly, truly I say unto you'. But now he not only says 'Amen'; he is the Amen. His ministry fulfils all the promises of God, 'for no matter how many promises God has made, they are "Yes" in Christ' (2 Corinthians 1:20). So then, his words are reliable because of his steadfast character. He is neither fickle nor capricious. No idle whim ever moves him to speak or act. He has never needed to retract or modify any statement which he has made. He is absolutely consistent.

Moreover, he is *the faithful and true witness* (verse 14; compare Revelation 1:5). Because his words are true, they are therefore trustworthy. 'We speak of what we know,' he claimed in his conversation with Nicodemus, 'and we testify to what we have seen' (John 3:11). Therefore his witness should be received. It is accurate and dependable.

Such is Christ, *the Amen, the faithful and true witness, the ruler of God's creation.* How can we ignore the advice of such a Being? He cannot lie. He knows and tells the truth. It would be the height of lunacy to disregard his counsel.

### The divine merchant

What then is his advice? *I counsel you to buy from me....* We pause again a moment. We must not miss the emphasis which is laid on the words *from me.* It was this above all that the Laodiceans had to learn. They considered themselves self-sufficient; they must humbly find their sufficiency in Christ. They were saying *I ... do not need a thing*; they must come to admit that their need was great and that only Christ could supply it. They said 'I am rich, I have acquired wealth, and I need nothing'. Jesus Christ had to humble that boastful personal pronoun and lay it in the dust, and say 'it is *from me* that your salvation comes'. He might have echoed God's words to Ephraim, 'your fruitfulness comes from me' or his own statement to the twelve, 'apart from me you can do nothing' (Hosea 14:8; John 15:5).

But why does he recommend the Laodiceans to *buy* from him? Can salvation be bought? No. Certainly not. It is a free gift to us because it was purchased by Christ on the cross. His invitation *buy from me* should not be pressed. He is doubtless using language appropriate to the commercially-minded Laodiceans. He likens himself to a merchant who visits the city to sell his wares and goes into competition with other salesmen. 'I advise you to forsake your former suppliers,' says the divine merchant, 'and come trade with me'. Perhaps also he is thinking of Yahweh's appeal: 'Come, all you who are thirsty,

**A young boy selling bread in modern Turkey.**

come to the waters; and you who have no money, come, buy and eat! Come, buy wine and milk without money and without cost' (Isaiah 55:1).

So Christ continues: *I counsel you to buy from me gold refined in the fire, so that you can become rich; and white clothes to wear, so that you can cover your shameful nakedness; and salve to put on your eyes, so that you can see* (verse 18). Here is welcome news for naked, blind beggars! They are poor; but Christ has gold. They are naked; but Christ has clothes. They are blind; but Christ has eye salve. Let them no longer trust in their banks, their Phrygian eye powders and their clothing factories! Let them come to him! He can enrich their poverty, clothe their nakedness and heal their blindness. He can open their eyes to perceive a spiritual world of which they have never dreamed. He can cover their sin and shame and make them fit to partake of the inheritance of the saints in light. He can enrich them with life and life abundant. In a word, he can save them. He has died for them and risen again. Through his death they can be cleansed, and through his living presence within them they can be changed.

### Two steps to take

But how could this come about? The Laodiceans must take two steps. The first is given in verse 19. The Lord Jesus goes on: *Those whom I love I rebuke and discipline. So be earnest, and repent.* The first step is repentance. Already Christ has called on those in Ephesus and Sardis to repent (Revelation 2:5; 3:3). The same message is addressed to Laodicea. There can be no glossing over this charge. The Christ who warns them that he will spit them out of his mouth if they do not stir themselves, nevertheless loves them. Indeed, it is because he longs to save them from final judgment that he now reproves and chastens them. They must *be earnest, and repent.* The tenses change significantly. Let them repent at once and irrevocably; then let them continue always to be fired with zeal. To repent is to turn with resolution from all that is known to be contrary to God's will. Like the Laodiceans we have to renounce the old life of easy-going complacency. Smug self-satisfaction is not appropriate in one who bears the name of Christ. Shallow piety never saved anyone. There will be no hypocrites in heaven. So we have to break with these things. We must spit them out of our mouths lest he spit us out of his.

If the first step is repentance, the second is faith. Exactly what the commitment is which the New Testament calls faith is now clearly and vividly described by Jesus Christ. *Here I am! I stand at the door and knock. If anyone hears my voice and opens the door, I will come in and eat with him, and he with me* (verse 20). This is a personal appeal. Although the words are addressed to the church, they apply to individual members of the church. *If anyone* ... Christ says. Our heart or soul is likened to a dwelling. Each of us likes to rule our own roost and be king of our own castle. But the living Christ comes to visit us. He who threatens that he may have to spit us from his mouth now stands on our front doorstep. He knocks. He wants to be admitted. It is a visit from the Lover of our soul. The love scene in the Song of Songs repeats itself. 'Listen! My lover is knocking: "Open to me, my sister, my darling, my dove, my flawless one ..." My lover thrust his hand through the latch-opening; my heart began to pound for him. I arose to open for my lover ...' (Song of Songs 5:2–5).

## Paupers to princes

If we do open the door of our heart to Jesus Christ and let him in, he will bring an end to our beggary. He will transform us from paupers into princes. He will cleanse us and clothe us. He will sup with us, and we shall be permitted to sup with him. The picture illustrates the shared joys of the Christian life, the reciprocal fellowship which believers have with their Saviour. That he should bid us come and sup with him is honour enough; but that he should wish to share our humble board and sup with us is wonder beyond our finite understanding.

We are not worthy that he should come under our roof, and will he sit at our table? Of this inward festive meal the Lord's Supper is the outward and visible sacrament. To eat bread and drink wine is but a physical representation of the spiritual feast with Christ and on Christ which his people are privileged continuously to enjoy. To kneel at his table in a church sets forth publicly our private supping with him in our hearts. And both the inward feast and the sacramental supper are a foretaste of that heavenly banquet which in the Book of the Revelation is called 'the wedding supper of the Lamb' (Revelation 19:9; compare Luke 22:30).

## The master of the house

But it is not merely for supper that Christ enters the human soul. It is also to exercise sovereignty. If he comes in to bestow his salvation, he comes in also to receive our submission. His entry is an occupation. He comes in to take control. No room may be locked against him. He has conquered us. He is the master of the house. His flag flies from our roof. This is what it means to be committed to Christ, and to be wholehearted in our allegiance to him. It is to surrender without conditions to his lordship. It is to seek his will in his word and promptly to obey it. It is not just attending religious services twice a Sunday or even every day, let alone on the major festivals. It is not just leading a decent life or believing certain articles of the creed. No, it is first to repent, turning decisively from everything we know to be wrong, and then to open the door to Jesus Christ, asking him to come in. It is getting our gold, our clothes and our eye salve from him. It is being personally and unconditionally committed to him. It is putting him first and seeking his pleasure in every department of life, public and private. Nothing less will do.

Whether we are hot, cold or tepid depends on whether we have opened the door of our personality to the Lord Jesus Christ. It is only the beginning of the Christian life; but it is an indispensable beginning.

## The prospect Christ offers

Like the previous six letters, the letter to the Laodicean church concludes with a gracious promise to the overcomer, to the man or woman, that is, who hears, heeds and obeys Christ's message. *To him who overcomes, I will give the right to sit with me on my throne, just as I overcame and sat down with my Father on his throne* (verse 21). This prospect exceeds in glory all the other promises to the overcomer. A throne is the symbol of conquest and authority. Jesus had promised the twelve that 'at the renewal of all things, when the Son of Man

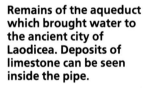

**Remains of the aqueduct which brought water to the ancient city of Laodicea. Deposits of limestone can be seen inside the pipe.**

123

**A street scene in modern Jerusalem.**

sits on his glorious throne', they who have followed him would 'also sit on twelve thrones, judging the twelve tribes of Israel' (Matthew 19:28). This pledge is now given to every faithful and overcoming Christian. As Christ overcame the world and the devil, and was exalted to the Father's right hand, so the Christian overcomer shall be honoured also. As Christ shares the Father's throne, so Christians will share Christ's. Exactly what authority will be entrusted to them is not disclosed, but in some way they will be given responsibility in the Kingdom of Heaven.

If we let Christ enter the house of our heart, he will let us enter the house of his Father. Moreover, if we allow Christ to sit with us at our table, he will allow us to sit with him on his throne.

### The great choice

Here then is the great alternative which confronts every thoughtful person. To be half-hearted, complacent and only casually interested in the things of God is to prove oneself not a Christian at all and to be so distasteful to Christ as to be in danger of a vehement rejection. But to be wholehearted in one's devotion to Christ, having opened the door and submitted without reserve to him, is to be given the privilege both of supping with him on earth and of reigning with him in heaven. Here is a choice we cannot avoid.

The last verse of the chapter reads: *He who has an ear, let him hear what the Spirit says to the churches* (verse 22). These words are repeated without alteration as a postscript to each letter. They are reminiscent of a characteristic expression which Jesus used during his public ministry: 'He who has ears to hear, let him hear' (see for example Mark 4:9). The phrase in Revelation is almost identical, and only adds *what the Spirit says to the churches.* The letters are dictated by Christ, but the message is the word of the Spirit. He who spoke through the prophets in olden days and through apostles in the New Testament revelation is now the agent of the Son's charge to the churches.

It is noteworthy also that although each letter is addressed to a different church, the concluding formula refers to *the churches.* The personal message to each is yet a general challenge to all. The message varies according to the circumstances of each congregation, but not according to the purpose of the divine writer. His will for his church is the same, for every congregation of every age and every place. It would be foolish to turn a deaf ear to this urgent message. *He who has an ear, let him hear what the Spirit says to the churches.*

*'There before me was a throne in heaven ...'*
Revelation 4:2

# Conclusion

Revelation 4:1–2

We have seen what Christ thinks of his church. We have considered the marks which should characterize it – love for Christ and willingness to suffer for him, truth of doctrine and holiness of life, inward reality and evangelistic outreach, with an uncompromising wholeheartedness in everything. We have watched the church hard pressed by sin, error and lethargy within, and by tribulation and persecution without. We have been introduced to the evil designs and deeds of the Nicolaitans, the Balaamites and the woman Jezebel, and behind them of Satan himself. We have caught many glimpses of the dilemma between Christ and Caesar which was being forced upon Asian Christians. It was hard for them to stand firm in the midst of opposition.

**The unchangeable throne**
But we cannot leave them thus. With chapter four of the Book of Revelation we turn from the church on earth to the church in heaven, from Christ among the flickering lampstands to Christ near the unchangeable throne of God. *After this I looked,* John writes, *and there before me was a door standing open in heaven* (Revelation 4:1). Through this door of revelation he looked, and his eye lighted on the symbol of the

---

### Revelation 4:1,2

After this I looked, and there before me was a door standing open in heaven. And the voice I had first heard speaking to me like a trumpet said, 'Come up here, and I will show you what must take place after this.' [2]At once I was in the Spirit, and there before me was a throne in heaven with someone sitting on it.

The Colosseum, Rome, one of the most impressive reminders of the might of the Roman Empire.

sovereignty of God. *There before me was a throne in heaven with someone sitting on it* (4:2).

The churches of Asia were small and struggling; the might of Rome seemed inexhaustible. What could a few defenceless Christians do if an imperial edict were to banish them from the face of the earth? Already the powers of darkness seemed to be closing in upon them. The hearts of Christians began to tremble like the trees of the forest in the wind.

Yet they need have no fear. At the centre of the universe is a throne. From it the wheeling planets receive their orders. To it gigantic galaxies give their allegiance. In it the tiniest living organism finds its life. Before it angels and human beings and all created things in heaven above and earth beneath bow down and humbly worship. Encircling the throne is the rainbow of God's covenant, and surrounding it are twenty-four other thrones, occupied by twenty-four elders, who doubtless represent the twelve tribes of the Old Testament and the twelve apostles of the New, and so the completed and perfected church.

### The church's security
These chapters of the Book of Revelation (4 to 7) leave us in no doubt about the security of the people of God. The Eternal

Father sits on his throne, surrounded by the worshipping host of heaven. The Book of Destiny is in the hand of Christ, and no calamity can befall humankind unless he breaks the seals of the book. Moreover the winds of judgment are not permitted to blow upon those who have been sealed by the Holy Spirit. These are the symbols of divine sovereignty. The church's security is guaranteed by the Holy Trinity.

So ultimately, when we have fought a good fight and finished our course, and, even if need be suffered death for the name of Christ, we shall emerge from the great tribulation and suffer no more. We shall join the church triumphant, the great multitude which no one will be able to count, drawn from every nation, tribe, people and language, and we shall stand with them before God's throne. The King of the universe will grant us refuge in the shelter of his throne, where we may see him and worship him day and night in his temple, and the Lamb turned Shepherd will lead us with the rest of his sheep to fountains of living water, where we may slake our thirst for ever at the eternal springs.